ALSO BY GAO YUAN

Born Red

LURE
THE TIGER
OUT OF
THE
MOUNTAINS

GAO YUAN

THE
THIRTY-SIX
STRATAGEMS
OF
ANCIENT CHINA

SIMON & SCHUSTER
New York   Sydney
London   Tokyo
Toronto   Singapore

SIMON & SCHUSTER
Simon & Schuster Building
Rockefeller Center
1230 Avenue of the Americas
New York, New York 10020

SIMON & SCHUSTER and colophon are
registered trademarks of Simon & Schuster
Designed by Edith Fowler
Manufactured in the United States of America
Illustrations © 1991 by Zheng Qinghua

10   9   8   7   6   5   4   3   2   1

Library of Congress Cataloging in Publication Data
Yuan, Gao
  Lure the tiger out of the mountains: the thirty-six
stratagems of ancient China / Gao Yuan.
     p.   cm.
  1. Strategic planning.   2. Marketing.   I. Title.
HD30.28.G36 1991   90-45480
658—dc20   CIP
ISBN 0-671-69489-8

To my second son, Gabriel Tianjiao Gao,
with the hope that his generation
uses this ancient military lore
to wage peace instead of war

ACKNOWLEDGMENTS

The primary inspiration for this book was my memories of my late grandfather, Fu Zhong. I first learned of The Thirty-six Stratagems as a child listening to his bedtime tales of the Three Kingdoms.

I thank my elder brother, Gao Han, an expert in military strategy and another beneficiary of Grandpa's stories, for his great help in the research for this book.

I also am grateful to Master Lao Xin, whose lectures on Taoism gave me much insight into life; David Packard, for his enthusiasm about my manuscript; Harold Leavitt, professor of psychology and organizational behavior at Stanford Business School, who encouraged me to find a publisher for it; Ted Polumbaum, for the many discussions and debates that invigorated my thinking; and Nyna Polumbaum, for linking me up with the right literary agent.

My thanks also to my agent, Faith Childs, for her support and professionalism, and to my editor, Bob Asahina, and his assistant, Belinda Loh, for their confidence in my work. Finally, I thank Judy Polumbaum for rearranging my prose with skill and care, and for adding a bit of wisdom of her own.

CONTENTS

SIX
STRATAGEMS FOR DESPERATE STRAITS

INTRODUCTION

THE AMERICAN DREAM says that anyone can build a successful life and career through hard work and thrift. But this simple prescription no longer works in today's complex world and cutthroat business environment.

Increasingly, Westerners are turning to Eastern wisdom for help in coping with the challenges and stresses of modern life. Some have taken inspiration from the tolerant and nonmaterialistic philosophy of Zen Buddhism. Others try to anticipate future twists and turns of their lives by tossing pennies and studying the interpretations of hexagrams in the Chinese classic *The Book of Changes* (*I Ching*). Some seek the keys to directing events in the links between laws of nature and laws of human behavior expounded by Chinese philosopher Lao Zi in *The Way of Power* (*Dao De Jing*), the classic text of Taoism. Still others have chosen to wage battle in accord with the advice of ancient Chinese military strategist Sun Zi, author of *The Art of War* (*Sun Zi Bingfa*).

This book introduces a compendium of ancient Chinese wisdom that is little known in the West—the time-honored Thirty-six Stratagems. In contrast to *The Art of War* and *The Way of Power*, these stratagems were authored not by a single genius, but rather by untold numbers of military leaders and tacticians, politicians, merchants, philosophers, writers, and even ordinary people. They were not set down all at once in one place but were elaborated, enriched, and perfected gradually over five millennia of wars, coup d'états, court intrigue, economic innovation and

15

competition, and even the development of the Chinese game of Go (*Weiqi*)—which, with 10-to-the-761st-power possible configurations, is far more complicated than Western chess with its mere 10-to-the-120th-power possible configurations.

The Thirty-six Stratagems are of practical use to anyone interested in understanding the dynamics of history, politics, business, and human relationships, and in enhancing his or her life or career. Taken singly, they provide explanations of phenomena as varied as international espionage, corporate takeovers, automobile accidents, and childhood nagging. They also offer concrete advice that can be applied to everything from courtship to salemanship, tennis to technology, and teaching to manufacturing. Whether you are starting a new venture or improving an existing one, whether you are on familiar ground or in unexplored territory, whether you are the underdog, one among equals, or on top of the heap, The Thirty-six Stratagems are certain to yield something of immediate relevance to your situation.

Taken as a whole, The Thirty-six Stratagems teach a way of thinking. They provide a means for comprehending other people's behavior, including both deliberate and inadvertent actions, and for analyzing all sorts of situations, those arising serendipitously as well as those emerging by design. Individuals who master The Thirty-six Stratagems will be equipped to develop solutions to all kinds of problems and adapt to all kinds of contingencies.

Even if you are one of those fortunate people who feel entirely satisfied with their lot in life, The Thirty-six Stratagems will prove enjoyable and enlightening reading. This book will lead you into the recesses of five thousand years of Chinese history, with its countless tales, both true and apochryphal, of human wit and folly, diligence and recklessness, fidelity and ingratitude, victory and defeat. These stories are drawn from twenty-four volumes of historical chronicles, literary classics such as the *Romance of the Three Kingdoms* (*Sanguo Yanyi*), and modern works, in-

cluding the writings of Mao Zedong—who used The Thirty-
six Stratagems masterfully in fighting Chiang Kai-shek and
the Japanese.

Readers who already are familiar with other Chinese
classics will find some familiar themes in The Thirty-six
Stratagems. For instance, the number thirty-six itself de-
rives from the philosophy of the unity of opposites, expounded in the *Book of Changes* as the notion of yin and
yang. Yin and yang are two complementary categories in
the universe; everything in the world is thought to belong
to one or the other. Yin is the female element, manifested
in earth, wind, water, and marshland and associated with
darkness and enclosure, while yang, the male element, is
manifested in heaven, thunder, fire, and mountains and
associated with light and openness. The ancient Chinese
considered schemes and stratagems, often planned and implemented in secrecy, to belong to the yin. The concept of
yin in the *Book of Changes* is represented by the hexagram
for "earth." This hexagram is composed of six lines, with
each line broken into two segments, resulting in two columns of six short lines, whose product is thirty-six.

The philosophy of unity of opposites appears throughout
The Thirty-six Stratagems. The principle that the interaction of yin and yang determines the development of events
is seen in the myriad of relationships explored in the stratagems—between offense and defense, strength and supple-
ness, regularity and surprise, void and solidity, the enemy
and oneself, guest and host, work and rest, and many more.

Another important principle of the unity of opposites is
that a quality or entity can transform into its opposite.
Given the appropriate circumstances, the weak can defeat
the strong, the small can surpass the big, and an enemy
can turn into a friend. The transformation may be un-
planned or inevitable: hippies turn into Yuppies; the sexual
revolution gives way to the AIDS era; and the nuclear arms
race brings about negotiations aimed at the ultimate elim-
ination of nuclear weapons. Or it may be the result of strategy by one or more parties.

Military history, politics, and business provide ample examples of human-engineered transformations:

• Witness Mao Zedong's rout of Chiang Kai-shek following World War II. When the showdown began, Chiang had eight million troops and several billion dollars' worth of U.S. military hardware, while Mao had fewer than one million troops armed with old Japanese rifles. Within three years, Mao mounted three major campaigns against Chiang, the largest wiping out more than half a million of Chiang's best troops. The outcome is well known: Mao set up the People's Republic of China in 1949, and Chiang fled to Taiwan.

• Mao and Richard Nixon's common interest in developing a countervailing power against the Soviet Union brought longstanding enemies together. Mao, having railed against "U.S. imperialism" for decades, invited Nixon, who had built a political career on anticommunism, to China in 1972. Thus the process of normalization of U.S.–China relations began.

• Through force of statesmanship and personality, Mikhail Gorbachev changed Americans' image of the Soviet Union. Ronald Reagan, who labeled the Soviet Union the "evil empire" at the start of his presidency in 1981, warmly received Gorbachev in New York in 1988, and New Yorkers gathered along Gorbachev's motorcade route to cheer him. Public opinion polls showed him ahead of then president-elect George Bush in popularity.

• Charles Wang, head of an obscure subsidiary of a Swiss electronics firm, was laughed at in 1983 when he talked about becoming the world's largest independent software producer. The company went on to swallow its parent and nearly a score of competitors and finally acquired its major rival. Today, Computer Associates International dwarfs even such software giants with household names as Microsoft Corporation and Lotus Development Corporation.

• Recognizing that two-thirds of the soft drinks consumed in the United States are cola drinks, the makers of

Seven-Up found a formula for success in the "uncola" position.

Strategy has long been associated with the battlefield, but the pinnacle of strategic attainment is to win without resorting to arms. As Sun Zi put it, "To subdue the enemy without fighting is the acme of skill."

Indeed, strategy alone may prevail where arms alone would fail. An ancient court official named Yan Ying was well aware of this. Yan Ying worked for the state of Qi during the Spring and Autumn period (722–481 B.C.) when China was divided into several kingdoms, each trying to swallow up the others. The following story shows how Yan Ying used the subtleties of diplomacy to fend off the larger and stronger state of Jin:

The king of Jin had sent an emissary named Fan Zhao to Qi to see whether Qi was vulnerable to attack. The king of Qi, not wanting to anger the more powerful state, threw a banquet for Fan Zhao. At the banquet Fan Zhao requested to drink from the king's wine cup, and the king agreed. However, Yan Ying grabbed the royal cup from Fan Zhao's lips and substituted another. Then Fan Zhao pretended to be drunk and requested that the royal orchestra play royal music to accompany his dancing. Yan Ying again intervened. Fan Zhao left the banquet in anger. The king of Qi was worried and scolded Yan Ying for offending the emissary, anticipating an invasion as a result. Meanwhile, Fan Zhao returned to Jin and reported that when he had tried to breach court etiquette, Yan Ying had seen through him right away. The king of Jin agreed that with Qi in such good order an invasion was ill-advised.

The sage Confucius, a child of four when this incident occurred, as an adult commented admiringly that Yan Ying had frustrated a plan for an invasion from thousands of miles away "without going beyond the banquet table."

Strategy can be vital in a disadvantageous situation, like that confronting the state of Qi. But it is essential even when one holds the advantage. The Thirty-six Stratagems are divided into six sets, the first three designed for use from positions of strength, the second three from positions of weakness. Specifically, the six categories are: (1) stratagems to be used when commanding superiority, (2) stratagems for confrontation, (3) stratagems for attack, (4) stratagems for situations of confusion, (5) stratagems for gaining ground, and (6) stratagems for desperate straits.

However, this classification was never meant to be rigid; on the contrary, over several millennia of practicing and refining these techniques, Chinese military strategists learned that the highest principle of all was flexibility. Sun Zi recognized the value of flexibility when he likened adaptability in warfare to the behavior of water, which changes its flow according to the ground. Lao Zi, the Taoist philosopher, recognized the power of flexibility when he observed that water is at once the most yielding of elements and the mightiest of eroding forces. Good strategists, like water upon rock, yield to the terrain in order to wear away the most unyielding of obstacles. They don't simply confine themselves to stratagems that ostensibly fit their circumstances, rather they mix and match according to actual conditions. You can combine several stratagems from the same set or use a blend of stratagems from different sets if need be. In short, the ultimate rule for applying these stratagems is to follow no rule.

This book devotes a chapter to each of The Thirty-six Stratagems. In the Chinese language, each stratagem can be summed up in a pithy three- or four-character phrase. For each one, the Chinese characters, as well as the pronunciation in the pinyin system of transliteration, are provided to give an idea of the ideographic depiction as well as of the sing-song intonation that are lost in English translation. The stratagems' historical and legendary origins are traced through ancient tales and anecdotes illustrating their use. Their enduring value as analytical tools and guides for action is illustrated with examples drawn from contemporary times and guidelines for how they might be used in working out careers, personal relationships, and other daily-life concerns.

ONE

STRATAGEMS
WHEN
COMMANDING
SUPERIORITY

These stratagems are the most straightforward and therefore the most easily seen through. To succeed with them, you often need to be in a stronger position to start with, and even then they may backfire. In general, they rest on an assumption of superior force—the resources to besiege others, the time and sustenance to relax while waiting for the enemy to tire, the manpower to pretend to attack in one direction while really attacking in another.

A familiar sight provokes no attention.
—*CHINESE PROVERB*

STRATAGEM

1

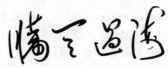

Man tian guo hai

Cross the sea by fooling the sky

SECRETS OFTEN HIDE in the open. In fact, the more obvious a situation seems, the more profound the secrets it may hide.

People tend to ignore the familiar. This is the principle behind the stratagem of crossing the sea by fooling the sky.

Chen Shubao, the last king of the short-lived Chen dynasty who reigned some fourteen centuries ago, was a victim of this stratagem. An accomplished poet and a connoisseur of wine, women, and music, Chen Shubao ran his court in a blatantly self-indulgent and extravagant manner. Even when listening to reports on state affairs from court officials and generals, he kept his favorite concubine on his lap.

What would become the Sui dynasty had consolidated

power in North China, and when Sui founder Yang Jian learned of Chen Shubao's dissoluteness, he decided the time was ripe to move across the Yangtze River and take the South. He put General He Nuobi in charge of the job.

The Yangtze's southern bank was heavily fortified, and He Nuobi ruled out direct engagement or a surprise attack. Nonetheless, he deployed forces along the northern bank, set up colorful tents and banners, and began to move large numbers of troops in and out.

Seeing all this activity, the Chen commander assumed an invasion was imminent. He put the entire defense corps on alert.

But the Sui troops did not attack, and after a while the Chen commander concluded that they were only conducting routine maneuvers. The Chen troops gradually grew tired of waiting for an enemy who did not come, and relaxed their vigilance.

On the first day of the lunar new year in 589, when Chen Shubao was still sleeping off a night of drinking, womanizing, and poetry reciting, He Nuobi mounted a surprise crossing of the Yangtze and invaded the capital of Chen, today's Nanjing. When Sui troops stormed the Chen palace, Chen Shubao took his favorite concubine and another young consort and jumped with them into a well. The well water was so shallow that none of them drowned; instead, they were discovered and pulled out. The concubines were executed and Chen Shubao was taken prisoner. Their hiding place went down in history as "the well of humiliation," which became a popular allusion in poetry of later dynasties.

The stratagem of crossing the sea by fooling the sky plays on the yin-yang relationship between overt and covert, regularity and irregularity, familiarity and surprise. Each element in these pairs can hide the other, and each can transform into the other.

The stratagem works because people expect secrets to be hidden. It is logical to think that such plans must be made and conducted in secrecy. Thus people tend to neglect open activities that hide underlying schemes.

The more ordinary an activity, the less attention it draws. People become inured to the commonplace: when you drive along a familiar route, your attention may flag; thus most car accidents occur near home. If your lover sends you roses every day, the gesture will become meaningless. Eating too much hot pepper will deaden your taste buds.

The wolf in the tale of "The Boy Who Cried Wolf" was a prime beneficiary of this principle. Once the townspeople had become used to the boy's false alarms, they ignored him when the wolf actually arrived to devour the sheep.

Hitler used this stratagem in the invasion of France during World War II. He deliberately leaked information on an imminent invasion twenty-nine times until British and French intelligence no longer took the leaks seriously, leaving France unprepared for the actual blitzkrieg.

On the other hand, the Allies used the same stratagem against Hitler. The 1944 landing at Normandy was preceded by several parachute drops of mannequins. The Germans had tired of the game and let down their guard by the time real paratroopers arrived.

In the early days of the Korean War, General Douglas MacArthur threw the North Koreans off the track by declaring that he was going to land at Inchon—and then actually landing there.

This stratagem appears in business whenever firms or executives achieve something by leading people to assume they will act in a predictable way and then doing something uncharacteristic. In the late 1970s the Belzberg brothers of Canada, having inherited the reins to their father's First City Financial Corporation, began showing up on the doorsteps of large U.S. companies brandishing minority shareholdings and threatening to take over. They quickly gained a reputation as raiders who could be bought off, and one company after another paid the Belzbergs greenmail—buying back the shares at a juicy premium over the market price. Wall Street therefore was unprepared for their surprise raid on Scovill Inc., which they acquired in 1985 with little resistance.

The stratagem of crossing the sea by fooling the sky also

may be seen in product modifications that loyal consumers would never suspect. When Japanese monosodium glutamate was not selling well, producers enlarged the little hole in the bottle from 1 millimeter to 1.5 millimeters in diameter. What person who used that bottle every day would imagine the little hole being secretly enlarged? Consumers unwittingly put more MSG in their food, boosting sales by 50 percent.

For those who want to make a mark in the business world or the political arena, this stratagem suggests that trying to impress others with an unending stream of ideas, proposals, and projects will accomplish little; whereas carefully chosen, well-timed moves will have more dramatic impact and greater chance of success. On the other hand, if you are in a situation where you don't want to be noticed, don't do anything extreme or out of character.

For managers, crossing the sea by fooling the sky suggests that the unrelenting taskmaster may be less effective in directing employees than the supervisor who puts on pressure selectively. Similarly, parents who constantly nag their children about chores, homework, and behavior will engender inattention, while those who make selective demands on their offspring may actually get results.

In daily life, this stratagem serves as a reminder that following predictable patterns that both you and those close to you feel comfortable with is a good way to maintain tranquility in personal relationships—and that doing something unexpected is a good way to inject excitement into a relationship that seems to be flagging.

> *He who knows the art of the direct
> and indirect approach will be
> victorious. Such is the art of
> maneuvering.*
> —*Sun Zi,* THE ART OF WAR

STRATAGEM

2

Wei wei jiu zhao

*Besiege the kingdom of Wei to
save the kingdom of Zhao*

TO ASSAULT a strong and cohesive enemy head-on is to invite disaster. The stratagem of besieging the kingdom of Wei to save the kingdom of Zhao advocates indirect confrontation.

Sun Bin, a descendant of the great military strategist Sun Zi and the man credited with preserving Sun Zi's *The Art of War* for posterity, used this strategy to rescue an ally from an invasion while settling an old score.

The original of Sun Zi's masterwork, written with brush pen on bamboo slats, is thought to have been destroyed when invaders burned down a tower where it was concealed in a hollow pillar. However, the knowledge contained in the treatise was passed down to Sun Bin. Sun Bin became a military adviser to the king of Wei, the strongest of seven feuding kingdoms during the Warring States period (403–221 B.C.). Pang Juan, chief military commander of Wei, was intensely jealous of Sun Bin's brilliance, and his envy soon led to murderous schemes. Intercepting and doctoring a letter from Sun Bin to his home state of Qi, Pang Juan convinced the king of Wei that Sun Bin intended to defect. The king ordered Sun Bin delivered to Pang Juan for punishment.

Pang Juan feigned surprise at the sight of Sun Bin in shackles and promised to appeal to the king on his behalf. He advised the king not to execute Sun Bin but merely to incapacitate him and still retain his services. Then he took credit for saving Sun Bin's life. He even pretended to cry as the prisoner's kneecaps were cut out and his face tattooed with the words "For carrying on illicit relations with a foreign state." (Carving out the kneecaps was one of five major forms of punishment in ancient China—the other four being cutting off the nose, castration, decapitation, and dismemberment by being roped to five oxcarts.)

Pang Juan subsequently asked Sun Bin to write out *The Art of War* with commentaries. Sun Bin readily agreed, still believing he owed his life to Pang Juan. But a sympathetic servant told Sun Bin that Pang Juan planned to let him starve to death once he had finished writing. Sun Bin pretended to go mad, and Pang Juan consigned him to a pigsty. There he languished until a delegation from Qi, ostensibly delivering a tribute of tea, smuggled him out in a cart. Another man stayed in the pigsty covered with filth until Sun Bin was safely home.

Sun Bin declined a high position in the Qi court, saying that when needed he would serve. The opportunity arose some years later when the Wei king dispatched Pang Juan to besiege the capital of the kingdom of Zhao, and Zhao turned to Qi for help. Instead of meeting Pang Juan's troops directly, Sun Bin orchestrated a diversionary attack on the capital of Wei, coupled with an ambush along Pang Juan's return route. The king of Wei sent an emergency message summoning Pang Juan back to defend Wei, and 20,000 Wei troops fell into the ambush. Pang Juan barely escaped. In the melee he caught sight of Sun Bin sitting in a wheelchair and realized that his rival had bested him.

The stratagem of besieging Wei to save Zhao plays on the yin-yang relationship between directness and indirectness, concentration and division, and solidity and void. It may mean concentrating one's forces to strike at the enemy's weakest point, taking advantage of an opponent's shortcomings, solving a problem by focusing on an aspect that seems tangential but is actually key, or deflecting a problem onto something or somebody else.

Mao Zedong often practiced this strategy in China's civil war. When Chiang Kai-shek's army advanced toward the Communist area, Mao sent troops where they were least expected—deep into Kuomintang-controlled territory.

Events in the U.S. presidential primaries illustrate the power of diversionary blows. Gary Hart's and Joseph Biden's candidacies for the 1988 Democratic nomination fell not to frontal assaults on their politics or capabilities but to revelations suggesting an extramarital affair and exaggeration of scholastic achievements.

Then during the final stages of the presidential campaign, Republican George Bush mortally wounded Democrat Michael Dukakis through skillful and selective manipulation of diversionary images. The symbol of the campaign became convict Willie Horton, who committed rape and murder while out of jail on furlough—in a program initiated *not* by Dukakis but by his Republican predecessor.

At the Iran-Contra congressional hearings in 1987, Oliver North parried attacks by repeatedly raising the issue of the "communist threat" in Central America. His skill in diverting attention from legality to ideology was reflected in his resulting popularity; in one opinion poll, 56 percent of respondents said that if they ran a business they would gladly hire him.

A business that wants to make inroads in an industry dominated by giants may find besieging Wei to save Zhao preferable to a direct challenge. It is suicidal to try to compete with IBM for the personal computer market; but one can avoid direct confrontation and carve out a specialized niche, as Sun Microsystems has done in the area of workstations, becoming No. 1 producer of linked office stations built around powerful minicomputers. Other Silicon Valley companies, notably Netframe Systems, are concentrating on specialized "server" computers designed to coordinate activity among networked PCs or workstations—a job formerly requiring adaptation of more general-purpose machines. And Apple Computer established its beachhead in the relatively neglected area of educational applications before branching out to compete with IBM for business clientele.

Similarly, the strategy of indirection is useful for the established business trying to ward off a challenge. When French tire manufacturer Michelin made inroads into the U.S. market with its new radial tire technology in the early 1970s, the U.S. manufacturer Goodyear responded with both technological improvements and a counterattack in the European market. When Michelin cut prices by 5 percent in Europe, Goodyear cut prices by 15 percent. The attack on Michelin's traditional territory helped Goodyear maintain dominance on its home turf.

Corporate lawyers are well aware that the best response to a lawsuit from a competitor may be a countersuit. After Atari Games filed an antitrust lawsuit against Nintendo, accusing the latter of improperly controlling the supply of game cartridges, Nintendo filed a countersuit charging Atari with breach of contract, trademark law violations, and unfair competition—thus forcing the rival to divide resources between offense and defense.

Children's television advertising has long relied on the stratagem of besieging Wei to save Zhao—entrancing the child with cereals, toys, or other products on the expectation that the child will find the way to the parental pocketbook. McDonald's and other fast-food corporations likewise snag parents via their kids by providing kiddie meals complete with kiddie toys. The child is the line of weakest defense, easily succumbing to the temptation of the latest Disney cartoon figure, Muppet pal, or "McNugget buddy." The child then works on the parents, presumably the line of strongest defense. Mom and Dad may think they have discovered a secret weapon—the promise of going to the local fast-food outlet for the latest offering if the child behaves, or the threat of staying home if the child misbehaves; but in fact the corporation is wielding the weapon.

Investigative journalists, detectives, and attorneys often use techniques of indirection to elicit information, knowing that difficult or sensitive questions may not be answered when asked point-blank. But even if you are not in these occupations, you may find yourself in adversarial situations in which besieging the kingdom of Wei to save the kingdom of Zhao is the only way to learn something you need to know.

Indirection may be employed in personal interactions for the sake of kindness as well. Americans tend to be straightforward, even blunt, in their dealings with others—in contrast to people from Asian cultures in which indirection is a common practice. But when you have something critical or unpleasant to convey, taking a circuitous route may soften the blow.

STRATAGEM

3 借刀杀人

Jie dao sha ren

Kill with a borrowed knife

IF YOU CAN CAUSE or convince someone else to do a difficult job, you may save yourself a great deal of trouble. Borrowing a knife to kill means making use of others' resources for one's own gain.

This strategy finds expression in the *Book of Changes*, hexagram number 41, which signifies a decrease or loss. When the top and bottom halves of the hexagram are reversed, it means an increase or gain. Loss and gain complement each other and can turn into each other.

During the Spring and Autumn period (722–481 B.C.), the king of the state of Zheng employed the borrowing strategy to pave the way for an invasion of the state of Kuai. He set up a sacrificial altar, beneath which he buried a name list of all the wise officials and brave generals of Kuai, plus descriptions of the rewards they would receive should Kuai fall. The king of Zheng then held a grand ceremony with animal sacrifices at the altar and made sure the king of Kuai learned of it. The king of Kuai obtained the list, suspected those on it of plotting against him, and executed every one of them. Shortly after that, Zheng conquered Kuai.

Military strategists throughout Chinese history have employed the stratagem of borrowing. Two famous adversaries of the Three Kingdoms period (A.D. 220–265) were masters of it: Zhuge Liang, who was a wise and loyal adviser to Liu Bei, the upright founder of the kingdom of Shu; and Cao Cao, the canny and merciless ruler of the kingdom of Wei.

Zhuge Liang borrowed another's strength to secure an important foothold in two key cities at the juncture of the three kingdoms—Shu, Wei, and Wu. The founder of Wu was Sun Quan. Knowing that Shu's forces alone could not defeat either Wei or Wu, Zhuge Liang advised Liu Bei to ally with Sun Quan. Liu Bei went along, forging the alliance by marrying Sun's sister! Then together Zhuge Liang and Sun Quan defeated Cao Cao at the decisive Battle of Red Cliff.

This by no means ended the battle of wits between Zhuge Liang and Cao Cao, however; their personal rivalry went on for many years, and the jockeying for power among the Three Kingdoms divided China for nearly half a century.

Cao Cao later tried to borrow Sun Quan too, promising him that if he could wrest one of the key cities back from Shu he could keep it. Sun Quan finally agreed. He would have to defeat Liu Bei's invincible general Guan Yu, and did so by sending an unknown commander against Guan Yu while another commander took the city by surprise. These events forced Guan Yu into a rout and ambush, after which he was decapitated. The Chinese people later turned the brave Guan Yu into the semimythological God of War, also called Guan Di.

Cao Cao employed the borrowing stratagem for pettier

purposes as well. Once he hired a talented but arrogant young man as a drummer at a banquet. When he asked the young man to change from his shabby clothes into a performer's costume, the new hireling stripped naked in front of the guests. Cao Cao refrained from ordering the musician's death and drawing criticism upon himself; instead, he sent the musician to a nobleman whom he knew was too short-tempered to tolerate such insouciance. Sure enough, the musician did not live long.

One ancient military treatise directed strategists to expropriate anything and everything from opponents—from officers and troops to money, materials, and wisdom. The ultimate art of borrowing is to make your opponent borrow what you need for yourself, or better yet, to borrow what your opponent borrowed from others for himself—without him even realizing what you are doing!

The author of the Ming dynasty novel *The Golden Lotus* (*Jin Ping Mei*), China's best-known work of erotica, did in an enemy with such malevolent artistry. It's said that after completing his manuscript, the writer soaked it in deadly poison and sent it to his adversary, an official who was an avid reader of pornography. In licking his finger to turn each page, the official ingested the poison.

There are countless modern examples of borrowing a knife to kill. Hitler used the method on the eve of World War II when he and his intelligence service provided the Soviets with trumped-up evidence that the Soviet marshal Mikhail Tukhachevskii was plotting to topple Stalin. As a result, the Soviets themselves executed Tukhachevskii and seven other generals whom the Nazis regarded as major obstacles to conquering Europe.

The organized-crime practice of hiring hit men is an obvious example of using others to do one's dirty work. The same idea holds in the case of nonmurderous but nonetheless shady tasks. One businessman who responded to a poll about whether he would hire Oliver North said yes, "if I had a dirty job to do and didn't want to do it myself. It sounds like he knows how to improvise to get the job done, without dirtying the hands of those who asked him."

In a broad sense, the stratagem of borrowing a knife to kill means making full use of others' resources for your own gains. This does not necessarily have to hurt anybody else, although it may fool a lot of people. For instance, during China's Cultural Revolution (1966–76), Mao Zedong's ambitious but ultimately unsuccessful struggle to generate continuous revolutionary spirit, a talented young poet wrote many poems under Mao's name. (Mao himself was a fine poet.) Few people remember the young author's name, but many former Red Guards can still recite some of his poems.

The leveraged buyout that came to dominate corporate acquisitions during the 1980s employs this strategy; it literally uses borrowed funds to take over a company. Junk-bond financing, which rests on unsecured, high-interest securities, is a variation.

Advertising commonly resorts to borrowing. Any celebrity who endorses, appears on behalf of, or performs for a product, company, or cause is a borrowed knife. Thus we have Michael Jackson and Madonna lending their allure to Pepsi, an unending stream of big names touting the virtues of the American Express card, President George Bush plugging for the United Way, and former president Ronald Reagan making a Red Cross appeal on behalf of victims of the 1989 San Francisco earthquake.

VIPs are not the only ones worth borrowing: charities and other worthy causes also may borrow images of the poor and downtrodden to strike a sympathetic chord among potential donors. One can borrow ideology, as in the attention-getting Apple ad showing the Macintosh computer alongside volumes by Marx, Lenin, Engels, and Mao. "It was about time a capitalist started a revolution," the ad explained. One can borrow allusions to anything—power, wealth, happiness, or sex.

In the practical world of business, companies may borrow from themselves: launching a new product under a strong existing brand name lends it instant recognition and a loyal clientele. So McDonald's contemplates expanding its menu with McPizza and McRibs.

Companies often borrow from one another, of course. Any new product success is bound to lead to copycats. But borrowing can be mutually beneficial as well. Companies that make software for IBM computers are borrowing from IBM's successes, but the wide availability of programs customized to IBM machines in turn promotes acceptability and sales of IBM's products.

The experience of Compaq, whose personal computers both imitate and rival IBM's, provides a textbook case of adaptive borrowing informed by business savvy. How has Compaq survived when its machines are priced far higher than comparable imports and clones? Simple—by consistently providing computers that outperform IBM's for about the same price. Founders Rod Canion and his two partners were the first to offer a portable as powerful as the IBM desktop machine on which it was modeled. On at least two occasions, Compaq beat IBM to market with computers using the latest, most powerful chips. Compaq made its own version of a new IBM machine that unlike IBM's accommodated old peripherals. Compaq did not think up the notebook-size computer, but was the first to introduce ones with hard disks.

On the surface, borrowing a knife to kill may seem too inherently manipulative to play a positive role in human relations. In actuality, this stratagem provides an important and essential means of adapting to new circumstances and dealing with new people. Common courtesy and cultural sensitivity require that "When in Rome, do as the Romans do"—or as the Chinese say, "Wherever you go, you should sing the local tune." Taking on the trappings of the environment is simply a form of borrowing a knife.

The stratagem also suggests ways to improve familiar relationships. The closest of friends may clash over personality differences that could be reduced through mutual borrowing. If you are a slob and your spouse is compulsively tidy, for instance, making an effort to acquire even a bit of the other's idiosyncracy will help you get along better.

STRATAGEM

4 以逸待劳

Yi yi dai lao

*Relax while the enemy exhausts
himself*

WHILE RESTING may give the impression of weakness or
laxity, in actuality it provides an opportunity to consolidate
strength. The stratagem of relaxing while the enemy exhausts himself is based on the principle that what appears
soft and pliable can also be strong and firm, whereas what
appears invincible may be weak. Countless examples are
found in nature. The supple bamboo stalk yields to the wind
and remains standing, while the mighty oak bough snaps.
Water conforms to whatever terrain it courses over, yet it
cuts through the hardest rock. Men surpass women in brute
strength, yet women have greater stamina and longer life
spans.

This stratagem plays on yin-yang relationships such as
firmness versus yielding, exertion versus rest, and attack

versus defense. It makes full use of time, territory, and tactics of surprise. It also is a psychological maneuver that takes the edge off the enemy's spirit.

Sun Zi believed that an army's morale is highest at the start of a battle. As the battle goes on, morale flags, and eventually the soldiers become dispirited and long to go home. Therefore a commander should avoid clashing with highly spirited fresh troops, striking instead after their enthusiasm and energies are worn down.

Sun Bin, military mastermind for the kingdom of Qi, also knew the value of exhausting the enemy. Twelve years after besieging the kingdom of Wei to save the kingdom of Zhao (see Stratagem 2), Sun Bin again besieged Wei to save another neighboring state. When Wei commander Pang Juan led his troops back to defend their home, Sun Bin withdrew and led the Wei forces on a wild chase lasting many days. At the end of the chase, Sun Bin settled final accounts with Pang Juan.

To lure Pang Juan on, Sun Bin used the trick of "reducing the number of stoves"—after the first day he ordered 100,000 campfires built on the Qi campsite, after the second day only 50,000 were lit, and after the third day just 30,000 were set. Pang Juan was overjoyed, thinking that the Qi soldiers were deserting. Confident of imminent victory over his archenemy, he led two columns of cavalry troops to advance on the Qi at the highest possible speed. But the Qi army continued to elude them, always half a day ahead.

By the time the Wei cavalry reached the narrow valley of Malingdao on a moonless autumn night, the troops were tired and hungry. Pang Juan ordered them to press on. Advancing through the valley, they passed a huge tree. Pang Juan went over to investigate a white patch faintly visible on the trunk. By torchlight he could make out the words "Beneath this tree dies Pang Juan, per order of Sun Bin."

Alarmed, Pang Juan ordered a retreat. But it was too late. A torrent of arrows descended from both sides of the valley, felling men and horses by the thousands. Severely wounded, Pang Juan slashed his throat with his own sword.

Military mastermind Sun Bin "waits while the enemy exhausts himself"; finally the treacherous Pang Juan, facing utter defeat, dies by his own hand.

This story illustrates Sun Zi's observation that "The army that reaches the battleground early and waits for the enemy is rested and thus gains the initiative, while the army that arrives late and throws itself into battle is fatigued and forced into a passive position."

Exhausting the enemy was one of Mao Zedong's favorite methods in his guerrilla war against Chiang Kai-shek. What Mao lacked in numbers of fighters and weapons he made up for in mobility, flexibility, and cleverness. His troops would draw Chiang's deep into difficult territory until they were physically and mentally depleted, and then deal the fatal blow.

A modern practitioner of relaxing while the enemy exhausts himself is corporate raider Sir James Goldsmith. Executives of the paper manufacturer Crown Zellerbach who tried to defend that company from Goldsmith's unfriendly overtures in 1985 remember his insidious techniques. "On a Friday or just before a holiday, he'd come in with a new proposal you had to deal with," recalls Zellerbach's former chief financial officer George James. "Then he'd go off on his yacht, leaving top management to wrestle with this for a week, without a holiday—and he'd come back all tanned and rested, and we'd be worn out and haggard." Goldsmith ultimately succeeded, acquiring majority control of Zellerbach and promptly selling its largest division to the Virginia-based James River Corporation.

Large corporations that sit back and let small entrepreneurial firms explore speculative innovations with unknown market potential are also using the stratagem of relaxing while the enemy exhausts himself. Small companies typically absorb much of the risk of early commercial innovation. Only after the feasibility of a project seems assured does big business with its superior resources, organization, marketing networks, production facilities, and research teams move in by acquisition or by entering the market directly. This process is evident in the microcomputer industry, where many innovations originate with small start-ups, and in biotechnology, to which large pharmaceutical concerns are relative latecomers.

In essence, this strategy advocates patience—always a fine principle to bear in mind when forming and dealing with personal relationships. Most parents know that a child in the midst of a temper tantrum cannot be reasoned with—in fact, trying to talk to the child is likely to infuriate him or her even more. But once the dust settles, you may find a chastened boy or girl who is surprisingly willing to acknowledge the error of his or her ways. Likewise if you are having a dispute with your boss, spouse, or friend, time may prove the best mediator. And in love affairs, advances upon someone whom you find attractive may drive him or her away, whereas a nonthreatening stance of neutrality, and even vague and mysterious disinterest, may attract the person to come to you.

*An enemy with troubles at home is
ripe for conquest.*
—*Sun Zi,* THE ART OF WAR

STRATAGEM

5 趁火打劫

Chen huo da jie

Loot a burning house

THIS STRATAGEM is based on the assumption that adversaries already mired in problems are easier to overcome than those with no such distractions. It advocates taking full advantage of your opponent's misfortunes, and even fostering troubles that will sap his strength and divert resources that otherwise might be directed against you.

A feud between Gou Jian, the king of Yue, and Fu Chai, the king of Wu, gave rise to a classic example of looting a burning house.

In 493 B.C. Fu Chai laid siege to Yue in an effort to avenge the death of his grandfather, who had been fatally wounded after attacking Yue two years before. Gou Jian survived by bribing the prime minister of Wu with eight beautiful women and a thousand ounces of gold. At the prime minister's urging, Fu Chai spared Gou Jian's life on the condition that Yue become a tributary state and Gou Jian and his wife personally serve the Wu court.

Gou Jian and his wife duly reported to Fu Chai on their knees, bringing along 330 courtesans and their entire trove of treasures as tribute. They were put to work tending the Wu stables. When Fu Chai went out in his horse-drawn coach, Gou Jian walked in front, swatting flies away from the horse's nose with a horsetail whisk.

Three years went by, and Fu Chai let Gou Jian and his wife go back to Yue. Gou Jian faithfully sent tribute to Fu Chai every year but vowed to avenge his humiliation. He had slept on a bed of twigs as a prisoner in Wu, and after returning home continued to sleep on twigs so he would not forget what he had suffered.

An honest and dedicated ruler, Gou Jian put great attention into improving production in his state. Fu Chai, on the other hand, became increasingly self-satisfied and dissolute. He built palaces and filled them with beauties brought from all corners of his empire. Gou Jian found him the most beautiful one of all, a woman named Xi Shi. She captivated Fu Chai, and he built her her own palace and held banquets there almost every night. Gou Jian also sent skilled craftsmen and fine timber to Wu to encourage the wasteful construction of useless buildings. In addition, he borrowed rice from Wu and repaid it with steamed rice which when used as seed by Wu farmers failed to germinate. Fu Chai grew increasingly unpopular as famine spread across the land.

Fu Chai's son recognized the dangers of neglecting affairs of state, and one morning the prince went to see his father to give him a roundabout warning. The young man was holding a slingshot and his clothes and shoes were wet. He said he had been in the garden and seen a cicada vibrating its wings and looking very pleased with itself, not noticing a mantis was about to prey upon it. The mantis, in turn, did not notice it was being watched by a sparrow. And the sparrow did not notice the prince aiming his slingshot. "I

Gou Jian and his wife, forced to bring tribute to Fu Chai, later get vengeance for the humiliation; after Fu Chai has become totally corrupt and spends all his time in frivolities with his consort Xi Shi, they take advantage of his heedlessness and "loot a burning house."

was only thinking about the sparrow, and failed to notice the pond under the tree, and fell into it," the prince said. For a moment Fu Chai appeared enlightened, but then he grew angry and dismissed his son's admonishments without further thought.

The year 477 B.C. was especially bad in Wu, with a drought so severe that not only the rice seedlings but also the crabs living in the paddy fields died. Rather than attending to affairs at home, however, Fu Chai led his army to the north to preside over a meeting of all the principalities in the region. Gou Jian made his move, launching an offensive and easily taking the capital of Wu. When Fu Chai returned and begged for clemency, Gou Jian refused, giving him the choice of being beheaded or killing himself. He chose to die by his own hand.

Throughout history nations have tried to foster the internal weaknesses of other nations in order to gain advantage. From the mid-1800s on, the Western-controlled opium trade fed the cravings of Chinese addicts and drained the state's treasury. In successive invasions the Western powers easily wrested privileges and concessions from the Qing dynasty until they controlled the major ports and the British got Hong Kong.

In the legal profession, the phenomenon of ambulance chasing is a form of looting a burning house. The concentrations of immigration lawyers in southern California and Texas are a somewhat less distasteful example of positioning to benefit from the difficulties of others.

In business, the stratagem arises whenever a company finds profit in responding to a social problem. The AIDS epidemic created lucrative new opportunities for drug companies, and when the Food and Drug Administration finally approved the drug AZT for therapeutic use, AIDS patients and their advocates objected vociferously to the high cost. In an all-too-rare example of response to public pressure, the manufacturer Burroughs Wellcome Company lowered the price from about $10,000 a year for a full-dose regimen to $8,000, and then $6,500.

There are ambulance chasers of sorts on Wall Street—the investment banks and financiers that specialize in discovering undervalued and poorly managed companies. Texas investor Robert Bass is known for spotting undervalued companies in turmoil, buying a hefty stake, and pushing for change. His acquisition, with two partners, of Taft Broadcasting Company was a case in point: Taft's problems included high overhead, declining earnings per share, stiff competition, falling advertising revenue, the legacy of having overpaid for a new acquisition of radio and TV stations, and the difficulties accompanying a push into movie-making and TV production.

The takeover of the Pillsbury Company by the British conglomerate Grand Metropolitan is a masterful example of looting a burning house. Grand Met attacked Pillsbury in late 1988 when the latter was most vulnerable—it had been through three CEOs in two years, its return on equity was low and falling, and franchisees of its largest subsidiary, Burger King, were in open revolt, complaining of undercapitalization. Grand Met went right to Pillsbury's home turf of Minneapolis to win over the financial and political communities there. Meanwhile, Pillsbury could neither obtain bank loans to fund a recapitalization nor lure any friendly suitors. Ultimately it sold itself to Grand Met.

People in the relatively new occupation of "failure specialist" build their careers on looting burning houses. Hired by companies in trouble, they look for ways to transform burdensome debt into equity and persuade creditors to accept less and wait longer. Some are arbitragers who buy scorned securities at a deep discount in hopes of wringing a premium from the company. These corporate turnaround artists do best when others are doing worst. They have so much business these days that some snub cases generating less than $200 million in fees.

The principle behind looting a burning house is seen frequently in electoral politics. Incumbents are most vulnerable to challenge when times are tough. Jimmy Carter took the blame for the economic recession during his tenure as president and lost his reelection bid; while his successor Ronald Reagan presided happily over a recovery and easily won a second term.

Similar things occur in the business world. It is not necessarily a bad thing if you work for a company in turmoil, for it's when things are going badly that opportunities for advancement open up.

In interpersonal relationships, the stratagem of looting a burning house reminds us that people are most fragile when confronting difficulties. Therefore you should avoid criticizing, challenging, or otherwise upsetting individuals whom you care about when they are in the midst of dealing with other problems.

> *The commander who knows how to attack makes his enemy not know where to defend.*
> —Sun Zi, THE ART OF WAR

STRATAGEM

6 罄東击西

Sheng dong ji xi

Make a feint to the east while attacking in the west

DIVERSIONARY TACTICS are common in warfare. In fact, making a feint to the east while attacking in the west is such an obvious way to fool one's enemy that, when used by the not-so-clever, it may backfire. Zhou Yafu, a commander of the Eastern Han dynasty (A.D. 25–220), is famed for having seen through this stratagem in quelling a rebellion against the throne.

At the time, China was divided into twenty-two fiefdoms ruled by quasi-independent princes and fifteen prefectures directly controlled by the imperial court. The Emperor Jingdi, alarmed by the princes' efforts to expand their powers, began to cut down their territory, prompting the ambitious Prince Liu Bi to join with six other princes in rebellion. As the princes advanced toward the capital, Jingdi turned to Zhou Yafu for help.

The emperor first wanted Zhou Yafu to rescue his brother, whom the rebels had besieged. Realizing the rebels were in high spirits, Zhou Yafu refrained from attacking them. Instead he sent mounted troops to the rear of the renegade forces to cut off their supplies, knowing that the siege could not continue if they were unable to replenish supplies of grain, fodder, and arrows. When Liu Bi realized this, he called off the siege for what he thought would be a quick and decisive battle with Zhou Yafu.

Instead of fighting, Zhou Yafu kept his soldiers inside their camp, protected by high ramparts and deep ditches. After several days, with supplies rapidly dwindling, the desperate Liu Bi ordered an attack on the encampment. When Zhou Yafu heard deafening battle cries and drumbeats coming from the southeast, he sent a small division to the southeast corner of the camp. He himself led crack troops to the northwest corner, having correctly interpreted the noise in the southeast as trickery designed to divert attention from where the rebels were really concentrating their force.

Zhou Yafu's aides, thinking that he was trying to escape danger, sneered at him—but not for long. Under cover of darkness, wave upon wave of Liu Bi's troops sneaked in from the northwest. When they were close upon the camp, Zhou Yafu ordered his men to let loose their arrows. Liu Bi's men, having expected no defense from these quarters, suffered heavy casualties and ran away in great disorder. Finally Liu Bi's grain supplies ran out and he had to withdraw. Zhou Yafu pursued. The hungry and exhausted troops under Liu Bi were easily overcome and the insurgent movement collapsed.

On other occasions, smart military strategists have used the stratagem of making a feint to the east while attacking in the west with great success. It was one of Mao Zedong's favorites and was expounded upon in detail in his essay "On Protracted War." The key is making sure that your opponent will not see through your fake moves. The stratagem is most likely to work in situations when the other side is in confusion and cannot figure out where your true target lies. It hinges on the creation of wrong impressions—making the enemy think you plan to do one thing when in reality you're going to do something else. The underlying principle is similar to the rationale of Stratagem 1, crossing the sea by fooling the sky, because both emphasize substituting the unfamiliar or unexpected for the familiar or anticipated. However, the actual tactics suggested by these two stratagems are different: whereas crossing the sea plays on hiding secrets in the open, feinting to the east employs directional deception. In crossing the sea, one lulls the enemy into a state of sensory numbness so he won't anticipate attack. In feinting to the east, one creates a false impression so the enemy will think the attack is coming from one place when in fact it is coming from another.

In the spring of 1798 when Napoleon was laying plans to conquer Egypt and then India, he threw the British navy off the track by disseminating false information that his fleet in the Mediterranean would enter the Atlantic Ocean and land at Ireland. Britain indeed prepared to intercept the French fleet in the Straits of Gibraltar. Instead, Napoleon's ships crossed the Mediterranean for Egypt. When the British discovered the trick, they sailed for Alexandria, getting there even before the French had arrived. The British then guessed that Napoleon would be landing in Constantinople and headed there, whereupon the French fleet made an effortless landing at Alexandria.

The American invasion of Grenada in 1983 employed the same sort of trick. First, word that an aircraft carrier and warships were being sent to the Mideast to assist peacekeeping troops in Lebanon was leaked to the press. In reality the fleet went to Grenada. With no advance warning, the occupation of the island proceeded quickly.

Making a feint to the east while attacking in the west is a ubiquitous offensive tactic in sports. Basketball players feint passes, boxers feint punches, and batters planning to bunt take a powerful stance to throw their opponents off guard.

A company trying to buy time as it develops a new product can throw the competition off the track by leaking word that it is working on something else. A diplomat trying to keep a sensitive diplomatic mission confidential can throw the press off track by creating a cover story that places him somewhere else.

Subtle diversionary tactics in business can further both individual and corporate interests where a direct approach would fail. Take a manager whose salary is tied to the market value of his company. Naturally he hopes that the price of the company's stock will go up. If his firm is undervalued, he has an incentive to let investors know. However, if he simply announces that the stock is undervalued and everyone should buy it, chances are people will think he is boasting and will do the opposite. Instead, he may take another tack by issuing more debt. Increased leverage implies a higher risk of bankruptcy, and since the manager would be penalized contractually if bankruptcy occurred, investors conclude that he has good reason to believe that things are better than the stock price reflects. By making capital structure changes to convey information about the profitability and risk of the firm, he obtains his well-deserved raise.

Credit-card companies make a regular practice of feinting to the east while attacking in the west when they emphasize low annual fees while downplaying finance charges. Consumers tend to be much more aware of the annual fee than they are of their monthly finance charges, yet finance charges are where they really take it on the chin: a study by Northwestern University professor Lawrence Ausubel showed that over a typical three-month period during 1983–87, the average credit-card rate fell only one-twentieth as much as other short-term rates.

Diversion is an old trick in pacifying children. Unfortunately as they get bigger they are harder to distract; and by their teens they know when you are purposely changing the subject. Nevertheless, diversion still works on adults in certain contexts, as long as your feint to the east is convincing and your attack in the west sufficiently obscured.

In a love affair, for instance, feigning slight affection for somebody else may arouse just enough jealousy in your true love to deliver that person into your arms.

As a psychological tool, feinting to the east while attacking in the west can help you put problems in perspective. When you encounter difficulties in work or daily life, if you first think about the truly serious problems of famine, war, and other hardships that afflict a good portion of humanity, your own lot will suddenly seem far easier to cope with. Or you might want to go further and take out from your busy schedule to volunteer in behalf of the poor, the sick, or the homeless. Chances are you will find that you can tackle conventional work and family responsibilities with even greater confidence and vigor.

TWO

STRATAGEMS FOR CONFRONTATION

Confrontation often involves two parties who are roughly equivalent in strength. Tipping the balance requires more deception, and thus more complexity. Stratagems in this set depend on stealth and trickery—making the enemy underestimate you, sneaky rear attacks, infiltration, and taking advantage of loopholes.

*Everything in the universe is
created from something, which in
turn is created from nothing.*
—*Lao Zi*, THE WAY OF POWER

STRATAGEM

7 茫中生有

Wu zhong sheng you

Create something out of nothing

THIS STRATAGEM plays on the yin-yang relationship between existence and nonexistence, truth and falsehood, substance and appearance, fullness and emptiness. If you can create something out of nothing, what looks like the bleakest of circumstances can yield success.

That is what happened when Zhang Xun, a valiant county magistrate of the Tang dynasty (A.D. 618–907), took on seemingly impossible odds to defend his city from troops rebelling against the imperial government.

Heading the rebellion was An Lushan, whose ambition was as great as his sexual prowess: he first usurped the Tang emperor's favorite concubine and then usurped the throne. One of An Lushan's supporters, a former Tang official named Linghu Chao, led 40,000 troops to besiege the city of Yongqiu, where Zhang Xun had a small armed force at his command. After forty days some of the city's residents were trading their children for food. But Zhang Xun refused to give in and had officers under him who wanted to surrender beheaded.

When the Yongqiu defenders ran out of arrows, Zhang Xun ordered people to make a thousand life-size straw figures clothed in black, which his soldiers let down over the city wall on ropes after dark. Linghu Chao's troops loosed tens of thousands of arrows at what they thought were escaping enemies. The arrows stuck in the straw men, and Zhang Xun's soldiers pulled them back over the wall. Only then did Linghu Chao realize that the figures in the night were dummies and cease the assault. By then it was too late—and Zhang Xun had gone from total lack of ammunition to plentitude.

Later that night Zhang Xun sent 500 of his bravest fighters down the ropes. Linghu Chao's side thought they were straw men again and paid no attention. Zhang Xun's men stormed the rebel camp, chopping off heads of slumbering enemy soldiers as though they were melons. The rebels were thrown into disorder and Linghu Chao had to order a retreat.

Thus Zhang Xun transformed a passive position into an active and potent one. His defense of Yongqiu was a major factor in turning the military situation in favor of the imperial army.

Another story about making something out of nothing tells how Cao Cao, a major player in the rivalry among the Three Kingdoms, kept thirsty soldiers from deserting during a prolonged march. Galloping to the top of a hill, he gazed into the distance and then shouted to his soldiers. "A plum orchard lies not too far ahead!" The soldiers' mouths began to water and the crisis was averted.

A fascinating example of how something can actually be made out of what might seem to be nothing is the Judeo-Christian concept of God. Some historians believe that what held the Jews together as a group after other Semitic peoples were overrun was the belief in an invisible god. All other groups had national gods embodied in images that lived in temples—and if the image was smashed and the temple razed, the god died out. The intangible Jewish God, being physically unapproachable, was thus indestructible. The same intangible power of the Christian God no doubt helps sustain Christianity as a potent force around the world today.

A variation of making something out of nothing is making others think you have nothing when in fact you have something. During the Korean War, Mao Zedong was able to make the United States seriously underestimate China's capacity to intervene. But even as General Douglas MacArthur was talking about imminent victory, more than 100,000 Chinese troops quietly crossed the Yalu River under the darkness of night.

Propaganda often consists of efforts to make something out of nothing. Fabrication may turn into reality; the lie repeated a thousand times ultimately may come to be accepted as the truth. However, propagandistic endeavors are most likely to succeed when they make a lot out of a little, building on preexisting attitudes to whip up fears, stimulate prejudices, or twist perceptions of facts.

Creating something out of nothing is a tried and tested stratagem in espionage. Perhaps the most successful intelligence coup of World War II involved the creation of a fictitious person—supposedly a British major whose drowned corpse was found by Spanish fishermen in 1943. So carefully had the British laid this plot that the major's death was even reported in *The Times* of London. Documents with the body indicated convincingly that the Allies were planning to invade Greece, information the Spanish promptly divulged to the Germans. In fact the invasion target was Sicily.

Some types of businesses are adept at creating something out of nothing, the car industry being a notable example. Automakers tout each year's models as "new" and "improved," but most of them merely have a different interior fabric, added pin stripes or body molding, or at most a stronger engine. A mere handful of the hundreds of models of cars and trucks can accurately be described as new—meaning they contain original engines, suspension, styling, or dimensions that are truly departures from the year before. Among 1990 models, for instance, GM's Mini Van, a couple of models of Honda and Nissan sedans, Chrysler and Mitsubishi sports coupes, and a few more importers' offerings were among the few genuinely new vehicles.

Creating something out of nothing may take the form of a sophisticated technique in advertising. Nissan launched its new upscale car division Infiniti with an advertising campaign intended to foster demand for a product without even showing it. The ads featured tranquil scenes and symbols, everything from rock formations to birds—but no cars.

Innovators are innovative simply because they create things where others never recognized possibilities. Presidential campaigns were no big deal until Theodore White wrote his first *Making of the President* in 1968 and turned the event into a media industry. Journalist Timothy Crouse went one better—*The Boys on the Bus*, his scrutiny of how the news media scrambled over every stump speech and party caucus, made coverage of the campaign coverage a trendy endeavor.

Brian Ferren has built a forty-person company in East Hampton, New York, on the proposition that there will always be demand for things that don't exist. He puts together things so new they don't even have names, from movie sets requiring special equipment or effects to multimedia interiors for shopping centers.

Of course, creating something out of nothing frequently manifests itself as counterproductive activity. One of Parkinson's laws, the Law of Triviality, predicts that the time spent on any meeting agenda item is inversely proportionate to the expenditure involved. In other words, people make mountains out of molehills all the time.

Creating something out of nothing also may backfire if

what has been created is a house of cards. Michael Milken, former "junk bond" chief of Drexel Burnham Lambert, acquired fame and fortune through his success at financing corporate takeovers using risky, high-yield securities. But after Milken was indicted on violations of racketeering and securities laws and his whole approach cast into question, it seemed that such transactions might become a thing of the past.

STRATAGEM

8 嗜渡陳倉

An du chen cang

*Pretend to take one path while
sneaking down another*

THIS STRATAGEM plays overt, predictable, and public maneuvers against covert, surprising, and secretive ones. It
means drawing attention to one route while developing
alternate routes, acting much like the wind, which when
blocked at the window or door still whistles through even
the smallest of cracks.

A famous ancient practitioner of pretending to take one
path while sneaking down another was commander Han
Xin. Han Xin helped Liu Bang set up the Han dynasty,
which ruled China for over four hundred years (206 B.C.–
A.D. 220).

The Han dynasty was the second to oversee a unified
China. The Qin dynasty was the first. Qin founder Ying
Zheng had conquered six contending states to establish that

first centralized empire in 221 B.C. Ying Zheng's contributions had been manifold: they included standardization of the country's written language, calendar, currency, weights and measures, and even the length of cart axles. But Ying Zheng was also cruel in the extreme: he ordered all books but those on medicine, agronomy, and science and technology burned and had 460 scholars buried alive. He and the son who succeeded him collected as much as two-thirds of the harvested crops in land rent. They forced 300,000 corvée laborers to build the Great Wall and another 700,000 to construct a palace, mausoleum, and funerary relics—including the famed terra-cotta warrior army that draws so many tourists to the present-day city of Xian.

Under such burdensome rule, the peasants rose in revolt. Armed with clubs and hoes, they marched toward the capital and overthrew the dynasty. Then a contest emerged between two rebel leaders—Xiang Yu and Liu Bang. Most of the populace favored Liu Bang because Xiang Yu had committed the same kind of cruel excesses as the overthrown rulers, such as luring 200,000 Qin soldiers who had already surrendered into a death trap and executing a scholar in a cauldron of boiling oil. But Xiang Yu was able to assert superiority for a time because his army was four times as large as Liu Bang's.

Xiang Yu declared himself the king of Chu and named Liu Bang the king of Han, confining him to a territory to the south cut off by a towering mountain range. Liu Bang pretended to be content with his lot, even burning the plank roads that crossed the mountains and constituted the only passage from his region to the outside. In reality, however, he was drilling his armies under the talented commander Han Xin.

Three years later Xiang Yu's general in the area, Zhang Han, discovered that Han Xin's men were rebuilding the plank roads. Zhang Han was amused, as only a small force would be needed to guard the outlet. Shortly thereafter Zhang Han was shocked to learn that Han Xin's troops had reached the north side of the mountain range. Rebuilding

The troops of talented strategist Liu Bang "pretend to take one path while sneaking down another"—a winding route through the mountains that enables them to launch a surprise attack.

the plank passageway was only a ruse; meanwhile, most of Han Xin's soldiers were making a forced march by night along a winding detour through the mountains. Zhang Han took his own life, and within another year Liu Bang had defeated Xiang Yu and reunified China.

The Allied landing at Normandy during World War II is a modern application of pretending to take one path while sneaking down another. The Germans never expected the Allied troops to cross the English Channel at that point and concentrated their main defensive efforts in the Calais area. The Allies did all they could to reinforce this misperception, and as a result the Germans were taken by surprise.

Politicians often use this stratagem in times of crisis. Some analysts believe that the British and Argentine governments went to war in the Falklands partly to divert public attention from domestic problems in those two countries. Both governments were able to recoup some public support by drumming up nationalistic feelings.

In business, the stratagem has proven to be a good marketing tool. Those ubiquitous sweepstakes conducted by magazine subscription agents are a case in point. The entry rules—if you bother to read them—make it clear that no purchases are required. But the mailings cleverly exploit our realism as well as our sense of fairness: we can't believe we'll get something for nothing, and neither do we think we should. Therefore many of us dutifully subscribe to at least one magazine as we try our luck—a magazine we probably never would have bought on direct appeal.

In advertising, the stratagem may appear in the use of small print—epitomized in the timeless George Price cartoon of a signboard bearing the huge message "95 cents" with a tiny "and up" in the corner.

In strategic planning, pretending to take one path while sneaking down another may be a roundabout route to long-term success. Xerox priced its earliest photocopying machine at an exorbitant $2.95 million. The intent was to encourage rentals and service contracts and thus build up a network of dependent customers.

This stratagem can provide direction for dealing with parents, friends, your spouse, or your boss if you want to pursue a project that you're sure is good but that everyone else thinks is insane. When the whole world seems thus arrayed against you, you need to give the appearance of compliance while going ahead and doing what you think is right anyway. For instance, the high-school senior whose parents object to his taking a year away from textbooks should dutifully complete all those college applications—even as he plots his travel route in Latin America. And the employee with a cost-saving idea that the boss doesn't buy may have to develop it at home.

> *A clam was sunbathing with its
> shell open when a crane came
> along and pecked at its flesh. The
> clam snapped shut, catching the
> crane's long beak. Neither would
> yield to the other. Finally a fisherman
> came by and caught both of them.*
> —CHINESE FABLE

STRATAGEM

9 隔岸观火

Ge an guan huo

*Watch the fires burning across the
river*

TO WATCH THE FIRES burning across the river means to let
your enemies destroy themselves. Another way the Chinese
express this idea is "Sit on the mountaintop and watch the
tigers fight."

This stratagem takes advantage of contradictions or fac-
tionalism within the enemy camp. It requires a passive
approach; one must wait patiently for the antagonisms to
erupt. The stratagem is reflected in the *Book of Changes*
hexagram number 14, meaning comfort, which implies that
you need not take any action but rather may sit back and
wait for comforting news.

The wily Three Kingdoms chieftain Cao Cao used this
stratagem to defeat the Yuan brothers—Yuan Tan, Yuan
Shang, and Yuan Xi.

65

No sooner had the three fought off an attack by Cao Cao than they began to fight among themselves. The eldest, Yuan Tan, was angry because their late father had named the middle son, Yuan Shang, his heir. Yuan Tan asked Cao Cao for help in claiming his succession rights. Instead, Cao Cao killed Yuan Tan and also vanquished Yuan Shang and Yuan Xi. Those two fled and appealed for help from the leader of a nomadic tribe in the northeast, Gongsun Kang.

Gongsun Kang faced a dilemma: he did not trust the Yuan brothers, having suffered repeated attacks by their father over many years. On the other hand, if he aided the two surviving brothers they might help him resist Cao Cao, whose generals were defeating one nomadic tribe after another. Gongsun Kang sent word to the brothers that he was sick while he dispatched spies to find out Cao Cao's intentions. In fact Cao Cao was not planning an attack. Learning of the Yuan brothers' appeal, he had decided to let Gongsun Kang deal with them.

Gongsun Kang finally summoned the Yuan brothers to his reception hall and invited them to sit down. When Yuan Shang asked if the chieftain might have cushions brought for the bare wooden bench, Gongsun Kang declared, "Your heads are about to travel ten thousand miles; what is the point of talking about cushions?" Whereupon soldiers leapt from their hiding places and chopped off the Yuan brothers' heads. A few days later Cao Cao received the two heads in wooden boxes. Cao Cao rewarded Gongsun Kang by proclaiming him a duke.

In line with the same stratagem, Japan bided its time while Chinese fought Chinese during the early 1930s. After Chiang Kai-shek's massacre of Communists in 1927, the struggle between the Kuomintang and the Communist Party grew increasingly bloody. With both sides crippled, Japan easily occupied Manchuria in 1931. Then Japan waited further as the Chinese civil war escalated and the Communists were driven out of their base area in the south and onto the Long March to the northwestern loess plateau.

At last Japan launched its overall invasion of China in 1938.

Reliance on watching the fires burning across the river is evident in the history of empire-building. From the fifteenth century on, while the princes and republics of Central Europe were squabbling and carrying out schemes of aggrandizement against one another, the Western Europeans, particularly the Dutch, Scandinavians, Spanish, Portuguese, French, and British, were extending their ambitions across the seas. Then while these powers contended over their overseas conquests, tsarist Russia expanded east.

The little guy can often reap unexpected benefits from letting bigger adversaries battle things out. We sometimes see this in the sports world: for instance, while world attention focused on the figure skating battle between Katarina Witt of East Germany and Debi Thomas of the United States at the 1988 Winter Olympics, putting enormous and unnerving pressure on both contestants, the relatively unnoticed Canadian Elizabeth Manley skated calmly to a silver medal.

In business, newcomers may reap advantages from a tussle between established adversaries. In the late 1970s when two U.S. companies were fighting over the similarity of the names of their bug killers—the Cal Mex Bug Destroyer, which used electricity, and the Calameks Bug Killer, which used an odoriferous chemical—Maebashi Industries of Japan quietly overtook both with sales of its sonic bug exterminator.

When factional battles break out within companies and other types of organizations, managers have a range of options for handling the situation, from dictatorial intervention to a hands-off approach. In some contexts, the most successful and popular administrators are those who let contenders slug things out to the point of irrationality and then step in as impartial mediators. This technique is particularly effective in settings rife with individualists, such as academic departments of universities.

Adults usually feel the impulse to separate children embroiled in a tussle or argument, but here too, watching the fires burn may be the best approach. Even preschoolers may be capable of thrashing things out themselves, and gradually they will learn the importance of discussion and compromise.

*The man with honey on his lips
hides murder in his heart.*
—CHINESE SAYING

STRATAGEM

10 笑里藏刀

Xiao li cang dao

Conceal a dagger in a smile

THIS STRATAGEM means winning your opponent's trust and acting only after his guard is down. The approach is exemplified by a Tang dynasty official named Li Yifu who gained a high post in the imperial court because of his ingratiating manner and clever way with words. Behind Li's gentle and friendly face were ambition, greed, and vindictiveness. He let his family members solicit bribes from people who wanted to buy official titles. He persecuted all those who crossed him—he could be smiling at a minister in the morning, and in the afternoon send that same minister to the execution ground.

For a long time the emperor would hear no ill of Li Yifu. When Li Yifu tried to gain the release from prison of a beautiful woman who had been sentenced to death, planning to take her as his concubine, the prison warden was blamed for the scandal. The warden hanged himself. When another official reported that Li Yifu was the real culprit, the emperor not only didn't listen but demoted the informer to a remote post.

Finally though, the emperor could no longer ignore the stories of Li Yifu's meanness and corruption. Li Yifu was banished to a frontier region, where he died in disgrace. A century later, the Tang poet Bai Juyi wrote of him: "The likes of Li Yifu are always smiling, and a dagger hides behind the smiles."

You may disarm your opponent with a smile, with gifts, or with any other seemingly conciliatory gesture. Only a month before the Japanese bombed Pearl Harbor, they sent an emissary who was married to an American to the United States to discuss the two countries' interests in the Pacific.

Corporate raiders never admit to being out for blood—they insist that they merely want to reward stockholders for the value of their companies. But when takeovers succeed, the raiders typically proceed to cannibalize their acquisitions, selling off the most lucrative pieces.

On a less insidious note, concealing a dagger in a smile may merely mean doing well by doing good. The Marshall Plan, which revived a devastated Western Europe after World War II, was one such triumph of American ingenuity. The U.S. economy had emerged from the war stronger than ever and needed new and bigger markets to maintain its growth. With the relatively small sum of $13 billion in grants and loans to its allies, the United States achieved both economic and political goals: it created a vast new market for U.S. goods in Europe as well as opportunities for U.S. multinationals to expand, while maintaining stability in Western Europe and preventing the westward expansion of Soviet power.

A longstanding form of doing well by doing good is the establishment of the nonprofit foundation, by which wealthy families and corporations give society a great deal while gaining prestige and tax breaks in return.

A relatively new example is the move by major pharmaceutical manufacturers to give away experimental drugs that don't have final government approval to victims of AIDS and other serious diseases. The companies claim to be acting out of humanitarian reasons, a claim tantamount to a smile. But they also have strategic aims—the goodwill gesture improves an image that is under assault by consumer critics, allows them to protect cost information since they are not selling the drugs, and gains them a jump on marketing if the drugs are approved for continued use. These purposes, while not murderous, are equivalent to the dagger.

At the level of everyday affairs, the stratagem of hiding a knife in a smile suggests that sometimes it is necessary to cast the negative as positive in order to make a job or a situation palatable. People can accept unpleasant tasks or unwelcome news if they are presented in the guise of something good—just as Tom Sawyer convinced others that painting the fence was fun.

STRATAGEM

11 李代桃僵

Li dai tao jiang

Sacrifice the plum tree for the peach tree

ONE SOMETIMES must make partial sacrifices for the sake of overall victory. This may mean losing a battle in order to win the war or making a concession in order to achieve the main goal. The Chinese saying "Give up a pawn to save a chariot" expresses the same idea.

Sun Bin, the great military thinker who escaped the cruelty of Pang Juan to serve his home state of Qi (see Stratagem 2), employed the stratagem of sacrificing the plum tree for the peach tree first on the racetrack and then on the battlefield.

Qi military commander Tian Ji often raced and bet on horses with the king of Qi, and almost always lost. One day Sun Bin went along. After careful observation, he worked out a formula to guarantee Tian Ji success. Tian Ji tried it out the next day.

Sun Bin had noticed that Tian Ji's horses lost by only a hair in all three competition categories. This time Tian Ji put his first-class horse in the second-class race, his second-class horse in the third-class race, and his third-class horse in the first-class race. Naturally Tian Ji lost the first-class race but won the other two. By sacrificing one race, he came out ahead overall.

When Sun Bin was planning to ambush his archenemy Pang Juan, Tian Ji wanted to use Sun Bin's horse-racing method—that is, to sacrifice his worst column to Pang Juan's best, use his own best column to attack Pang Juan's middle column, and use his medium column to attack Pang Juan's worst column.

Instead, Sun Bin engineered a plan that took advantage of the mountainous territory to stall for time. First, Tian Ji's worst column went against Pang Juan's best, and his medium against Pang Juan's medium, while his best made a quick and decisive attack against Pang Juan's worst, wiping it out. Then Tian Ji's best joined his medium column to overpower Pang Juan's medium column. Finally these two columns joined Tian Ji's worst, and together they defeated Pang Juan's best. Although Tian Ji's worst column suffered many casualties, his troops were able to concentrate superior forces in the three successive stages of the battle, ensuring overall victory.

The stratagem of sacrificing the plum tree for the peach tree plays on the yin-yang relationship between superiority and inferiority, strength and weakness, the overall situation and the local situation, and sacrifice and gain. It requires a careful balancing of partial benefit and overall benefit, as well as of short-term versus long-term returns.

In warfare, this stratagem is not for the faint of heart. The price of success may be heavy losses, as with a Soviet crossing of the Dnieper river during World War II when two battalions were sacrificed in order to draw German fire north of Kiev and enable other forces to cross south of Kiev. The sacrifices may raise hard moral questions, as with the German attack on Coventry. The British government knew the attack was coming, having recently cracked

German codes, but decided not to deploy any defenses for fear of alerting the Germans to the new decoding capabilities. Thousands of civilians were killed.

Using this stratagem in business also takes resolve. Contradictions between short-term interests and long-term goals frequently arise in the business world. The Securities and Exchange Commission requirement of quarterly reporting and the quick-return orientation of Wall Street analysts and stockbrokers promote the short-term view. The benefits of product development, planning, and installation of new manufacturing facilities or entry into new markets may not be seen for some time. But the ultimate success of an enterprise depends more on such long-term projects than on quarterly earnings.

Voluntary sacrifice of short-term or local benefits to secure long-term, overall gains has been a key to Japan's industrial success. The difference between Japanese and U.S. approaches is exemplified by the case of semiconductors. U.S. chip makers, under pressure to minimize short-term losses, lay off workers when market demand for one generation of chips dwindles and have to gear up again to produce the next generation. Japanese companies hold on to workers and move right into next-generation production.

The lesson has not bypassed U.S. companies entirely. Texas Instruments priced low and sustained losses in the early stages of market development, eventually becoming profitable as smaller competitors dropped out. But big and prosperous firms have the clear advantage: it is hard to sacrifice the plum tree for the peach tree without a highly profitable product line in place to compensate for investment in areas that show losses. Witness IBM, which built its electronic computer business on the basis of its dominance in the electromechanical punch-card machine business. And even big firms must use the strategy with care—not like Xerox, which dissipated profits from its success with copiers into all sorts of unprofitable ventures, including trying to compete with IBM.

Compared with manufacturers, service industries may

find sacrificing the plum tree for the peach tree less painful because the net benefits are more immediately evident. Greyhound Lines, for instance, periodically lowers bus fares in accord with this stratagem. It did so three times in 1989 to woo back travelers disgruntled by rising airline fares and weary of driving. The company found that a 1-percent price cut typically produced up to a 3-percent increase in sales of same-day tickets and up to a 2-percent increase in advance ticket sales.

In the era of merger mania, sacrificing the plum for the peach may mean accepting the lesser of two evils. Directors of companies that are targets of unfriendly takeover attempts go hunting for "white knights," hoping to safeguard as much of their interests as possible rather than lose everything.

Sacrificing the plum for the peach also applies to striking a balance between diversification and concentration. Companies that diversify to spread risk may find themselves spreading their forces too thin. International Harvester tried to compete simultaneously with Ford and General Motors in the heavy truck sector, with John Deere in the mature and cyclical agricultural equipment sector, and with Caterpillar in construction equipment. As the second or third player in each area, the company could not be strong overall.

The conglomerate form of merger, which peaked in the United States during the 1970s, led to a high rate of business closings. Individual companies might benefit from short-term tax write-offs, but the trend was bad for long-term productivity and the nation's industrial health. The pitfalls of conglomeration are better recognized today than they used to be. However, a company can fail even in what appears to be a natural extension of its business. IBM bought Rolm for $1.5 billion as part of its thrust into the telecommunications sector and sold it to Siemens A.B. of West Germany four years later, when it was losing $100 million a year.

The dangers of concentrating on short-term local interests to the neglect of long-term, overall prospects are aptly described by ecologist Garrett Hardin as the "tragedy of the commons." Each farmer entitled to use common pastures will benefit individually by adding to his herd until the overgrazing that results from this pursuit of self-interest destroys the pasture that supports them all. Indiscriminate use of resources could spell destruction for everyone.

Even as modern communications continue to compress time and space, this realization of global limits is enlarging the time frame and geographic scope in which businesses operate. In the name of "corporate responsibility," business planners today must balance expensive investments in waste recovery systems and pollution controls against the long-term social good.

Many grains of sand piled up a pagoda make.

—*CHINESE SAYING*

STRATAGEM

12 順手牽羊

Shun shou qian yang

Take the opportunity to pilfer a goat

THIS STRATAGEM means taking advantage of opportunities as they arise. Not even the most minor mistake on the part of the enemy should escape attention. Every small slip by the other side can be turned into at least a small gain for you.

The quintessential use of this stratagem comes from the tale of Wu Qi—also called Wu Zi, a military strategist of the Warring States period who is often mentioned in the same breath as the great Sun Zi.

Wu had a checkered personal history: as a child, he ran away from home when his mother criticized him for frivolity and vowed never to return until he was a supreme commander or prime minister. As a student of Confucianism in the kingdom of Lu, he was driven out by his tutor for not being filial enough—when his mother died, he had cried briefly and then gone back to his books as if nothing had happened. When the kingdom of Qi attacked the kingdom of Lu and the king of Lu hesitated to appoint him chief commander because his wife was a member of the Qi royal family, he chopped off his wife's head and presented it to the king.

The king of Lu was not terribly happy about Wu Qi's particular way of proving himself but now understood that this talented man might defect to the other side if he didn't get his way. So Wu Qi was named chief commander after all, and he successfully repulsed the Qi invasion. Later though, he did defect; unable to shake the habit of angering his patrons, he went first to the kingdom of Wei and then to the kingdom of Chu.

The Chu king Daowang appointed him prime minister and encouraged him to pursue far-reaching political reforms. Wu Qi emphasized the rule of law, streamlined the bureaucracy, and abolished inheritance of titles by nobles beyond three generations, transferring the benefits to meritorious soldiers instead. Chu rapidly rose to become the most feared power among the warring states.

During the twenty-one years of Daowang's rule, nobody dared attack Chu. Once Daowang died, however, Wu Qi faced an assault from the nobility who had lost their titles. The king was not yet in his coffin when the nobles broke into the palace and started a rampage. They pursued Wu Qi into the royal chambers, arrows flying from their bows. Mortally wounded, Wu Qi jumped onto the king's corpse and held it tightly as the rain of arrows continued. By the time he was dead, the king's body also bristled with arrows.

Wu Qi's behavior may have seemed puzzling, but its purpose soon became clear. When Daowang's son mounted the throne and began an investigation into his father's death, he followed the letter of the law that Wu Qi had helped establish. That law made mutilation of the king's body punishable by death. Thus members of seventy noble families were executed for this offense. Wu Qi had availed himself of a final opportunity to avenge his own death.

The farsighted Wu Qi "takes the opportunity to pilfer a goat"; he
clutches the body of his king as his rivals rain arrows upon them,
knowing that even after he is dead these usurpers will be penalized
under law for desecrating the royal corpse.

Taking the opportunity to pilfer a goat is not common in conventional military action, but the stratagem is essential to guerrilla warfare. Small, poorly equipped forces cannot afford to let any chance to trouble the enemy slip by. Mao Zedong noted this in a pithy sixteen-character formula: "When the enemy advances, we retreat; when the enemy stops, we harass; when the enemy is exhausted, we attack; when the enemy retreats, we pursue."

In a competitive business environment, it is important to be alert to others' mistakes and oversights. The Japanese knew this when they stepped into the gaps left by U.S. producers in the consumer electronics field. Ingenious entrepreneurs have made fortunes by identifying needs that nobody else recognizes exist—who would have thought that cardboard sunshields for car windows would take off the way they have? And those who identify deficiencies in popular new products have it made—such as the software wizard who wrote a program to make laptop cursors larger just as laptop computers were taking hold.

Among those who made millions by filling niches overlooked by others: Sam Moore Walton, who amassed a fortune from his Wal-Mart discount chain concentrated in Sunbelt towns; J. R. Simplot who, with an eighth-grade education, made his fortune by selling 700 million pounds of French fries a year to fast-food outlets; and young James Jaeger, who developed a radar detector to alert speeding motorists to the police.

Whittle Communications Corporation specializes in slicing "niche" audiences out of an already fragmented media market. The Tennessee company roiled the communications industry with its magazine for doctors' offices and its TV channel for schools. Then it came up with a slick national-style magazine to be distributed exclusively through beauty salons. A copycat competitor, Communications Venture Group, planned to fragment the market even more with six different bimonthly issues addressing different subjects, to be circulated in beauty salons run by department and specialty stores.

The message of these business success stories is simple: Never disdain small opportunities. The national U.S. consulting firm Bain and Company has built this principle into its customer-recruitment strategy. As part of its efforts to develop long-term relationships, Bain likes to take on small assignments that have the wholehearted backing of the client's top executive and the potential to produce spectacular results. The hope is that such small jobs may be parlayed into big accounts.

Large companies that aim to provide something for everyone cannot ignore small opportunities either. Chrysler chairman Lee Iacocca has observed that in the United States, the rich get richer even during a depression, and they'll always want luxury cars. However, the industry also must address the budget-conscious end of the market by offering small, fuel-efficient cars.

Pilfering a goat is a useful stratagem for career advancement. It does not mean brownnosing; rather it means taking advantage of every opportunity to make yourself useful—and preferably indispensable.

But the stratagem is a two-edged sword when it comes to interpersonal relations. Used negatively, pilfering a goat can damage personal relationships. For instance, if you avail yourself of every opportunity to criticize your spouse, he or she is likely to take offense at the nitpicking. Positive pilfering, on the other hand, can greatly enhance personal interactions. If your chronically rude child comes out with a "please," you should praise him or her to the skies; children respond well to positive reinforcement of these small signs of civility. And noises of approval are no less appreciated by adults; it seems big people crave positive feedback as well.

THREE

STRATAGEMS FOR ATTACK

Attack tends to be the most difficult proposition in warfare because it exposes you to the enemy's firepower. Most casualties occur in attacks. Stratagems in this set try to minimize exposure through techniques ranging from surveillance and concealment of intent to subtle lures to direct strikes.

One can win without a fight.
—Sun Zi, THE ART OF WAR

STRATAGEM

13 打草惊蛇

Da cao jing she

Beat the grass to startle the snake

DURING THE TANG DYNASTY there lived a greedy county magistrate named Wang Lu. People in his district, certain that he was misappropriating public funds, submitted a complaint to him charging his bookkeeper with embezzlement. Without thinking Wang Lu wrote on the complaint, "By merely beating the grass, you have startled the snake hiding within."

This stratagem plays on the yin-yang relationship between direct and indirect approaches to problems. Under some circumstances, beating around the bush works better than hitting home. By striking at an ancillary target, you can startle your enemy into divulging crucial secrets. Sometimes you can make your opponent believe

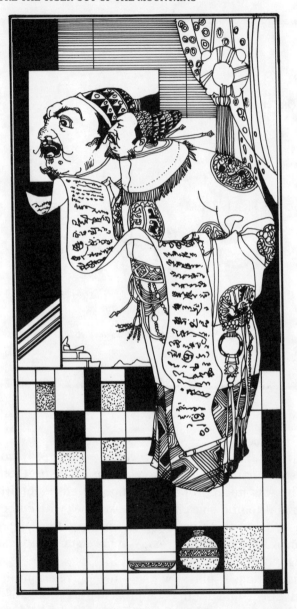

The greedy official Wang Lu recognizes that his constituents, in handing him a petition complaining about his subordinate, are really criticizing him—they are "beating the grass to startle the snake."

that you are closing in, and he'll more readily give himself up.

Beating the grass is also a way of getting the jump on an enemy who you think will attack you. Another historical example illustrates the dangers of not doing so. In 627 B.C. Mugong, the king of Qin, decided to launch a sneak attack on the kingdom of Zheng, ignoring the protestations of his top adviser Qianshu, who said that a surprise attack would be impossible because of the distance involved. Qianshu wept as he sent his troops off. Stealth proved impossible and the troops had to turn back. Qianshu also had predicted that they would fall prey to ambushes from the rival Jin army on the way home. The Qin soldiers might have beaten the grass to startle those in waiting but failed to heed the warning and were wiped out.

Sun Zi recognized the importance of beating the grass in his discussion on surveillance. He advised provoking the enemy and studying his response before launching a real offensive. This is what Britain and France did in 1956 when they dropped a batch of dummy paratroopers on the port of Said after Egyptian president Nasser had reclaimed sovereignty over the Suez Canal. After the extent of Egyptian firepower was revealed, the real airborne troops struck and took the port.

This stratagem emerges frequently in diplomacy and politics in the practice of floating "trial balloons." Henry Kissinger, while serving as secretary of state under Richard Nixon, was the master of this technique: having cowed journalists into obscuring his identity behind the label of a "senior official," he would leak information about his own activities, for which he wasn't held to account.

In business, beating the grass to startle the snake comes in handy in the initial stages of negotiations. It may take the form of careful listening and probing, good methods for gauging the other party's interests and intentions. Another business application of beating the grass involves jumping the competition in announcing a new product so that your competitors will be startled into divulging details

of their competing products before they are really ready—
and giving you a better idea of what you'll be up against
while you work out a marketing strategy.

Market research and test marketing are a mode of beating
the grass; the objective is to assess consumer reaction to
new products or services. And companies sometimes try
false moves in an effort to provoke competitors into a response that will reveal marketing strategies or technological advances.

Journalists often use the stratagem of beating the grass
to startle the snake. Muckraker Jessica Mitford recom-
mends starting an interview with an "unfriendly witness"
with easy questions in order to lull the subject into a con-
versational mood that predisposes him to reveal more. Investigative magazine writer Ramsey Flynn tries to
psychologically surround his sources by letting them know
who else he's been talking with; the result is that they think
he knows more than he actually does, and they tend to
proffer more information. Reporter Robert Scheer, in his
famous interview with Jimmy Carter, had not intended to
explore the question of adultery when Carter, as an after-
thought at the tail end of the session, volunteered the admission of having lusted after women other than his
wife.

A variation of beating the grass is to delay the grass-
beating so that the snake will not be startled. Law enforce-
ment officials may use this technique when they follow the
activities of a suspect; rather than flushing him out right
away, they gather more and more evidence to make a
stronger case. Similarly, a journalist on the track of a political scandal may postpone interviews with the principal
figures until they have committed enough transgressions
to make the story airtight.

The stratagem of beating the grass to startle the snake
suggests that you can sometimes conquer one problem by
addressing a different problem. If a teenager is doing poorly
at school, an assault on his or her homework habits may
be fruitless, while an effort to boost the child's self-esteem

through counseling may be reflected in better academic performance. Likewise, beating the grass to startle the snake means that one can learn much about people from indirect evidence. The best test of a lover, for instance, is not the other person's overt expressions of fidelity but whether he or she comes through for you in a crisis.

> *If you lack the proper title, people won't listen to you; and if they don't listen, your orders won't be carried out.*
>
> —*Confucius*

STRATAGEM

14 借尸还魂

Jie shi huan hun

Raise a corpse from the dead

THIS STRATEGY advocates making use of others. It is reflected in the *Book of Changes* hexagram number 4, meaning ignorance, which suggests that you can control people who lack the capability, intelligence, or knowledge to resist manipulation.

Raising a corpse from the dead goes back to the waning days of the Eastern Han dynasty (A.D. 25–220). Following the death of Emperor Lingdi, a bloody struggle ensued until the son of one of the late ruler's concubines ended up on the throne. Because the new emperor Shaodi was but a teenager, his uncle He Jin took charge of state affairs. When ten powerful court eunuchs spread a rumor that He Jin had murdered the empress dowager in the succession struggle, He Jin resolved to get rid of them and summoned a local strongman named Dong Zhuo to the capital to help. But before Dong Zhuo reached the capital of Luoyang, the eunuchs had killed He Jin in a trap.

Dong Zhuo saw a golden opportunity to usurp power from the declining dynasty. First he ordered the execution of every beardless male commoner in the capital. Before long he deposed Emperor Shaodi, put a nine-year-old puppet prince on the throne as Emperor Xiandi, and had himself named prime minister. He often appeared in court with his sword, executed officials under him at will, and soon became hated for his arbitrary and bloodthirsty behavior.

Cao Cao of Three Kingdoms fame (see Stratagem 3), then an up-and-coming military official, tried to assassinate Dong Zhuo but had to flee after the attempt failed. Subsequently Cao Cao helped organize an expedition against Dong Zhuo, whereupon Dong Zhuo killed the deposed emperor and forced the new emperor to move the capital from Luoyang to Changan (present-day Xian). Then some of Dong Zhuo's generals rebelled and took Xiandi hostage. They began to fight one another, kidnapping the young emperor back and forth. Finally Xiandi called on Cao Cao, who led 50,000 troops to defeat the rebel generals and escorted Xiandi back to Luoyang.

Later Cao Cao moved the capital again, forced the emperor to appoint him prime minister, and consolidated power in North China. However, Cao Cao's dream of reunifying China and becoming emperor himself was never realized. Liu Bei, another warlord, frustrated his southward advance and took over southwest China. Thus the famous Three Kingdoms period began.

The saga of the Eastern Han demonstrates how time and again, ambitious officials manipulated underaged rulers for their own purposes. He Jin and the eunuchs all sought to use Shaodi. Dong Zhuo, the generals, and Cao Cao treated Xiandi as a corpse to be raised from the dead, using the young monarch's status to realize their own agendas.

The same stratagem is evident in the Japanese occupation of northeast China in the 1930s, when Japan exhumed the still-living corpse of China's last emperor, Pu Yi, to serve as titular head of the puppet regime of Manchukuo. Pu Yi was the last heir of the last imperial dynasty, the Qing, which had been overthrown two decades before.

The U.S. government is sometimes criticized for using Third World strongmen to prop up its own interests around the world—the shah of Iran was a notorious corpse, even while alive, and others have included Anastasio Somoza of Nicaragua and Ferdinand Marcos in the Philippines. The Soviet Union supported a puppet government in Afghanistan, and the Vietnamese had its client regime in Cambodia.

Advertising may make use of corpses by borrowing the reputation of one product to advance the status of another. An example is the positioning of Yugoslavia's low-priced compact Yugo automobile. This car was presented as not only inexpensive and economical but also dependable through an association with the VW bug. A television commercial pointed out that the demise of the beloved basic bug had left "an emptiness in the hearts of America." Such back-to-basics nostalgia was the theme of several late 1980s Madison Avenue ad campaigns for products as diverse as magazines and whiskey.

The resurrection of old favorites is also reflected in Gillette's recent introduction of a new permanent razor following a decade in which disposable plastic was king. The trouble with disposable razors is that they are expensive to make and generate little profit. The company was banking on the maturation of buyers of the throwaways, which tend to be popular among men under thirty.

Raising corpses from the dead is a phenomenon often found in the informal cultural lore of corporations. Corporate culture is defined in part by semilegendary stories about the pathbreaking activities of founders and other luminaries. Apple Computer today is a member of the computer establishment, but its identity has been shaped by tales about the wild and crazy geniuses who founded it in a garage and the rambunctious, semiautonomous team of "pirates" who developed the Macintosh.

Although we seldom realize it, we often resurrect corpses in our choice of friends and lovers. Close relationships often hinge on surrogacy—how well a "significant other" fulfills the role of sibling confidant, or of Mom, or of Dad—or all of these! This tendency can become pathological, especially if it is one-sided. Such is the case, for instance, if one partner takes responsibility for everything while the other shirks it, as with parent and child. However, if the roles are shared and traded off, with each person able to be supportive and dependent or tender and tough, as circumstances require, this can only enhance the partnership.

> *Good opportunities are not as important as favorable terrain.*
> —*Mencius*

STRATAGEM

15 调虎离山

Diao hu li shan

Lure the tiger out of the mountains

RATHER THAN PLUNGING into dangerous and unfamiliar territory to reach an adversary, it is better to make him come out to fight you. Luring the tiger out of the mountains means drawing the enemy out of his favorable natural conditions in order to make him more vulnerable to attack. This idea is reflected in the *Book of Changes* hexagram number 39, which means obstruction and incorporates the elements of plains and mountains—the former easily traversed, the latter crossed only with difficulty.

This stratagem calls for consideration of geography, which the Three Kingdoms military strategist Zhuge Liang identified as one of three major factors in winning a war (the other two were opportunity and popular support) and Sun Zi regarded as one of five (along with climate, commanders, discipline, and popular support). It also calls for consideration of the nature of the beast—tigers, for instance, do well in mountainous areas but lose their edge in rivers, while a man-eating shark that wreaks havoc at sea can do little damage on land.

A military commander of the early Eastern Han period, Gen Yan, employed this stratagem to defeat two brothers leading separatist forces, Fei Yi and Fei Gan. Gen Yan led troops to surround a city held by Fei Gan and ordered them to make obvious preparations for an attack. While they felled trees to fill the moat around the city wall, Gen Yan's very best troops hid in the hills. When Fei Yi passed by with reinforcements to defend his brother, Gen Yan launched a surprise attack. Fei Yi was killed and his head brought to Fei Gan on a pole. Their morale shaken, Fei Gan's men deserted in large numbers and Fei Gan fled the city.

An extension of luring the tiger out of the mountains is to lure him into *your* mountains, putting him at even more of a disadvantage. In the American Revolution, British soldiers accustomed to fighting in conventional battle formation on flat, open territory could not stand up to colonial minutemen taking potshots from behind trees. Mao Zedong's guerrillas always set up their base areas in remote and forbidding mountainous areas that were familiar to them, and where Chiang Kai-shek's forces found themselves helpless in spite of having far superior numbers and equipment.

In international diplomacy, the head of state who can convince other heads of state to pay court to him wins the most points. The most even-handed summits are of course those that take place on neutral ground. Richard Nixon's journey to China in 1972, though a high point in Nixon's political career, put him in slightly subservient standing relative to Mao Zedong. Deng Xiaoping scored another coup when Mikhail Gorbachev agreed to come to Beijing in May of 1989—although unfortunately for Deng, the reception was upstaged by the massive demonstrations in Tiananmen Square.

A common tactic in political campaigns is to avoid the

territory where one's opponent is strong while luring him out to where he is on shaky ground. During the 1988 presidential campaign, George Bush avoided minefields such as the budget deficit and the Iran-Contra scandal upon which Michael Dukakis could score points and instead attempted to undercut Dukakis's record on crime, abortion, and other inflammatory issues.

Politicians can consolidate control by luring others into difficult positions. Many Western observers were amazed when Gorbachev, even while faced with strikes and nationalist unrest, engineered a purge of conservatives from the Soviet politburo in the fall of 1989. Gorbachev had isolated his rivals by giving them dangerously unpopular responsibilities. Viktor Chebrikov, a former KGB chief who had overseen security, was blamed for the country's sharp rise in crime and the decision to deploy troops against demonstrators in Tbilisi while Gorbachev was on a trip to Cuba and Britain. Viktor Nikonov had shared responsibility for the country's beleaguered agriculture with Yegor Ligachev. Ligachev was thought to be Gorbachev's prime adversary remaining on the politburo—and exceptionally vulnerable since now he alone had to shoulder blame for poor harvests and food shortages.

According to the stratagem of luring the tiger out of the mountains, people are most arrogant and confident in their home settings, and inviting them elsewhere should lessen their resistance to any requests you might have. Thus you may make more headway by taking your boss out to lunch to discuss a career move than by making an appointment to see him in his office. If you want to impress someone, take him or her to a special place you know well. And taking your spouse out of the house and into a dark movie theater is a wonderful way to rekindle romance.

To seize something, one must first thoroughly endow it.
   —Lao Zi, THE WAY OF POWER

STRATAGEM

16 敧撟故纵

Yu qin gu zong

Snag the enemy by letting him off the hook

THE STRATAGEM of snagging the enemy by letting him off the hook is used in the interests of avoiding bloodshed. Allowing a strong enemy to escape often works better than trying to corner him and provoking a desperate fight.

This approach is expressed in the *Book of Changes* hexagram number 5, which represents the concept of waiting and advises that one confronted with peril should not strike until success is assured.

The most famed practitioner of this stratagem is Zhuge Liang, the revered prime minister and brilliant military planner of the kingdom of Shu during the Three Kingdoms period.

Zhuge Liang was a master of psychological warfare. At no time were his skills better demonstrated than in the period following the tragic death of the Shu emperor, the suicide of the empress, and the ascendancy of their youthful and inexperienced son to the throne. To consolidate Shu rule during this difficult transition, Zhuge Liang let an adversary off the hook not just once, but seven times!

Many local strongmen and tribal leaders in the southwest part of Shu had rebelled after the emperor's death, and Zhuge Liang had managed to retake all but one of the insurgent regions. The remaining rebel leader was Meng Huo, a courageous chieftain with a large following in what is today's Yunnan province. Zhuge Liang realized that mere force would be fruitless against such a popular leader; instead, he had to win Meng Huo's loyalty.

What ensued was a series of captures and releases that proved Zhuge Liang to have the patience of a saint. Initially Meng Huo was captured in an ambush. The captive remained defiant, and Zhuge Liang released him. Then Meng Huo's own generals, resenting their leader's ingratitude, tied him up while he was drunk and personally delivered him to Zhuge Liang. Zhuge Liang again let Meng Huo go.

In the third encounter, Meng Huo sent his brother with gifts for Zhuge Liang and followed up with a nighttime attack. He found only his brother in a drunken stupor, reeling around an empty camp. When Zhuge Liang's troops burst out from hiding, Meng Huo fled to a nearby river, where Shu soldiers in disguise tied him up as he boarded a boat. Zhuge Liang freed him again.

In the fourth confrontation, Meng Huo assembled an army of more than 100,000 men from other tribes. The Shu troops retreated across the river and Meng Huo's pursued but halted to rebuild a bridge. Meanwhile, the Shu built a new bridge downstream, recrossed the river, and attacked the tribal warriors from behind. Meng Huo ended up trapped in a pit at Zhuge Liang's feet, but Zhuge Liang released him once more.

Another chieftain loyal to Zhuge Liang turned Meng Huo in. Zhuge Liang freed him for the fifth time.

After a series of additional battles, Meng Huo's brother-in-law pretended to turn Meng Huo in. When Zhuge Liang found their concealed weapons, he chastised Meng Huo for his trickery and let him go for the sixth time.

Meng Huo was captured yet again after rushing to the aid of troops trapped in a long, narrow valley. Offered freedom for the seventh time, he finally broke down and pledged his loyalty to the kingdom of Shu.

In another tale of letting the enemy go in order to catch him, the marquis Zhi Bo demanded land from the nobleman Wei Huan Zi. Wei Huan Zi complained to a friend, who advised compliance, saying, "The marquis is insatiably greedy. If you give him land, his greed will grow. He'll blackmail other nobles for more land. Then the nobles will unite against him." Wei Huan Zi followed this advice and sure enough, the marquis's greed kept growing, the other nobles joined forces to defeat him, and they divided his land among themselves. Wei Huan Zi not only recovered what he had lost—he gained more; in fact, his fiefdom expanded into one of the seven powers of the Warring States.

The stratagem of snagging the enemy by letting him go plays on the yin-yang relationship between give and take. Its success is based in part on the principle that one should never press the enemy too hard. In *The Art of War*, Sun Zi observes that an enemy with all escape routes cut off will fight wildly; therefore, any encirclement should leave a gap so the enemy won't feel determined to fight until death. Child-rearing experts similarly advise that when exercising discipline one should leave the child a way to redeem himself; otherwise the youngster will become totally intransigent.

Mao Zedong used this strategy against his greatest internal foe in the so-called Xian incident of 1936, in the midst of China's war of resistance against Japan. Two of Chiang Kai-shek's own generals had seized Chiang in an effort to force him to lay off his Communist rivals and concentrate instead on driving out the Japanese. Mao saw that killing Chiang would not be in the best interests of national unity against Japan and sent Chou Enlai to negotiate a united front policy allowing for Chiang's release—confident that once the Japanese were defeated, there would be plenty of time to handle Chiang.

After the Japanese surrendered, the civil war resumed. Again Mao let Chiang have his way for strategic purposes: when Chiang's army came to attack the Communist base area of Yanan, the Communists simply gave it up. "To give in order to take" was how Mao put it. Within a few years Mao had taken the whole country.

Sometimes one lets the enemy go now in order to catch him later. Other times, the act of letting the enemy go and the act of snagging him are one and the same. Apparent surrender is actually victory. For this to occur one must lay the psychological groundwork, inducing the target of the strategy to attach value to the surrender. This approach lies behind playing hard to get in a love affair.

Sun Microsystem's version of empire building revolves around letting the enemy off the hook: instead of guarding proprietary secrets, America's largest producer of computer workstations does whatever it can to spread them around. Sun's pragmatic chairman Scott McNealy operates on the assumption that only the big will survive in the computer industry, and growth for his company depends of the willingness of software companies to write programs for his machines. So Sun invites everyone from AT&T to the entire nation of Japan to buy its technology. Almost anyone can license Sun's basic software and the superfast microprocessor that is the brain of its flagship workstation. If enough manufacturers build Sun clones, the thinking goes, the software companies will have to take notice and the programs they write eventually will make Sun's machines the industry standard.

To this day, people still wonder about the public outcry that met Coca-Cola's move to match the sweetness of Pepsi with a revised formula, followed by the return of the Classic Coke to a near-orgy of consumer joy. The company reinvigorated its old market even while extending its product line, and while Coca-Cola maintains that the whole furor was unanticipated, it certainly looks like a classic case of surrendering to consumers in order to catch them. Within three months of the original formula's revival, the company reported that sales of its three sugared colas (including Cherry Coke) were running 10 percent higher than the previous year.

Reminiscent of the Coke tale is the comeback of the "Banquet beer" label on Coors beer. When Adolph Coors Company changed its beer subtitle to "Original draft," taking a cue from Miller Brewing Company's success with a campaign to emphasize its draft beer, many Coors loyalists complained. So alongside the new label the company reintroduced the original one in the Coors strongholds of El Paso and Southern California. Thus it made peace with old customers while still attracting new ones.

In late 1988 the French drug manufacturer Groupe Roussel Uclaf achieved a victory with two surrenders. Company officials insist it was by accident but they could hardly have planned it better.

The company had just put its new abortion-inducing drug RU 486 on the market, to the delight of public health workers and family planners and the dismay of abortion opponents. Potential sales were great—China, the world's most populous country, had already authorized the use of the drug. But the company's majority shareholder, a German chemical giant, became worried about boycott threats against its U.S. subsidiary. Uclaf caved in to pressure and announced it was withdrawing the drug.

The announcement coincided with a meeting of the World Congress of Gynecology and Obstetrics in Rio de Janeiro, where physicians were hailing RU 486 as a great breakthrough. Its withdrawal was resoundingly decried. The French government intervened and ordered Uclaf to reverse its decision. The company, relieved of the moral burden, gave in again and resumed marketing the drug.

> The kingdom of Jin wanted to
> attack the kingdom of Chouyou,
> but there was no direct route. So
> Jin cast a great bronze bell as a
> gift for Chouyou. Chouyou built a
> road to transport the gift from Jin,
> and then Jin troops came down
> the road and conquered Chouyou.
> —CHINESE TALE

STRATAGEM

17 拋磚引玉

Pao zhuan yin yu

Cast a brick to attract jade

CASTING A BRICK to attract jade means luring your opponent with something minor in order to obtain major reward. The principle is simple: You can't catch a big fish without bait. But what kind of bait to use and how to cast it are more complex. Whether the lure is a "sugar-coated bullet" or a Trojan horse, it must appear attractive or valuable to your adversary.

In 700 B.C. the kingdom of Chu used this stratagem to overpower the kingdom of Jiao. After Chu troops had tried without success to attack the Jiao capital, Chu withdrew. A few days later, a large group of woodcutters collecting firewood for the Chu encampment appeared outside the south gate of the Jiao capital. They chopped down many fine trees and carried them away. The commanders of the

Jiao army were enraged and ordered soldiers to pursue them. More than thirty woodcutters were caught, and their capturers rewarded.

The next day when another group of woodcutters appeared, all the Jiao soldiers rushed out to catch them without even awaiting orders, eager as they were for more rewards. Then Chu troops hidden in the hills on the other side of the city stormed the north gate. The Jiao troops were defeated, and the king of Jiao was forced to sign a humiliating peace treaty. (This incident, in addition to illustrating the stratagem, added one more idiom to the rich vocabulary of Chinese—"Concluding a treaty with an enemy who already has reached the city wall," which means bowing to the inevitable.)

Casting a brick to attract jade is a way to bring suspected secrets to light. Following the bombing at Pearl Harbor, U.S. intelligence believed it had figured out the code name for Midway Island from intercepted Japanese cables. Just to make sure, the Americans cast out a brick in the form of a cable reporting a shortage of water on the island. Shortly thereafter, that message appeared in Japanese communications. The confirmation of the code name enabled the United States to anticipate and fend off a Japanese attack on the island.

Many a spy has fallen prey to the stratagem of casting a brick to attract jade. During the 1970s the Chinese discovered that a Chinese citizen named Li was spying for the Soviets. Li agreed to cooperate with Chinese intelligence in exchange for lenient treatment. Without revealing that Li had been caught, the Chinese had Li contact the Soviet embassy in Beijing in his usual manner and arrange to deliver information. When three Soviet officials arrived at the meeting point in the northeast suburbs of Beijing, thousands of Chinese militiamen hiding in nearby fields emerged and surrounded them. The next day the Soviet spies were expelled.

Casting a brick is always a devious tactic but sometimes done with noble goals. A poet named Chang Jian who lived during the Tang dynasty was a great admirer of his famous contemporary the poet Zhao Gu. When he learned that Zhao Gu would visit Suzhou, he went to Lingyan Temple there and wrote two lines of verse on the wall. When Zhao Gu arrived and saw the unfinished work—even the simplest poem required four lines—he felt compelled to add two more wonderfully crafted lines. That poem is still famous today.

America's fast-food industry has discovered how to cast bricks in the past few years with the introduction of children's meals. What entices your kids to Wendy's is not the food but the dinosaur stuffed into the box along with the hamburger and fries. Any promotional gimmick that costs a company little but induces consumers to open their wallets is a brick that attracts jade.

Modern managers concerned with building and maintaining a motivated, committed, and happy work force must be cognizant of the whole range of human needs, and particularly higher-level needs for security, social interaction, self-esteem, and self-fulfillment. Many of America's most successful companies address these higher aspirations when they cast their bricks. Charles Wang of Computer Associates International supplies his employees with free breakfast and on hot days rides a cart through headquarters delivering ice cream. Hewlett-Packard holds monthly birthday parties for employees born in that month. Recognition, respect, and the opportunity to feel part of a group encourage loyalty and productivity.

A variation of casting a brick to attract jade is the technique that social psychologists call "foot in the door," or "taking a foot after gaining an inch," as it is called in Chinese. Beginning with a small request in order to gain compliance with related larger requests, this technique is based on the theory that people are more likely to accept the larger requests if they already have agreed to intermediary positions. If your son asks you to tell him five stories at bedtime, you will probably refuse—but when he follows one story with a request for "just one more," you may end up telling him five.

In pricing, companies use this stratagem to coax comsumers into making a small fixed investment that will be followed by a large variable investment. Polaroid prices its instant cameras low so consumers will buy them without thinking about the cost of film that follows. By the time purchasers realize that each ten-pack of film costs half as much as the camera, it is too late; and they continue to buy the film to justify the original purchase.

Another lucrative approach is to lure customers into complementing a large initial investment with not-so-small, add-on investments. Thus the cost of a new $15,000 coupe easily escalates to $18,000 when one adds a stereo, air-conditioning, power steering, power brakes, a sunroof, and so on. The buyer may feel happy about his purchase, but you can be sure the dealer feels even better. Ford's Mustang, in addition to representing a stylistic and engineering breakthrough, achieved immediate financial success due to this phenomenon: promoted as a sporty yet practical and economic car when introduced in 1964, the Mustang carried a relatively inexpensive price tag of $2,368. People not only bought them in record numbers; they eagerly tacked on accessories from white sidewalls and radios to automatic transmissions and tachometers, spending an average of $1,000 each on options!

Businesses also are casting a brick to attract jade when they put resources into creating a captive or addicted clientele. Apple Computer has been very successful in getting college students and professors addicted to the user-friendly Macintosh by donating systems to colleges as well as providing educational discounts.

But freebies need not always be so grand: one possibly apocryphal story has it that a Japanese company gained a multimillion-yen equipment order from a Chinese unit by giving out some free ballpoint pens. Almost 3 percent of Japan's gross national product is said to be spent on gifts, entertainment, and related activities seen as essential to the conduct of business.

Public relations firms often cast bricks to attract jade in their dealings with the press. Publicists involved in high-stakes business deals customarily release information to reporters on a selective basis, depending on their sense of how hard or soft the journalists will be on the client. In return, the firm may expect to extract some favors in the future—perhaps information from well-informed reporters or an article on another client.

One wonders whether financial institutions were not casting a brick to attract jade when they began to offer automated teller cards. In the long run, automation of transactions saves the institutions time and money—yet now that customers are addicted to the cards, some banks are starting to charge hefty user fees.

In family, friendship, and professional relationships, this stratagem reminds us that a little can go a long way. Casting the smallest brick—a compliment, a hug, a useful suggestion, a minor contribution to the day's chores such as washing the dishes or vacuuming the rug—will attract the jade of gratitude, goodwill, and respect.

If you are trying to succeed as an employee or a student, you can rise above the rest of your group if you distinguish yourself just once—by resolving a problem, answering a hard question, acing a test. Studies have shown that once your supervisors or teachers see evidence of your competence or intelligence, that impression will color all their subsequent dealings with you.

If you want to maintain family harmony, a brick you should cast every year is recognition of birthdays. The importance of birthdays is supposed to diminish as we age—but woe to the spouse who ignores one! Flowers, dinner, a movie can win peace for a year. This is beginning to apply even in China, where traditionally birthdays are marked with nothing more than a bowl of noodles (symbolizing longevity). Children's birthdays are still no big deal, but now as people grow older, their children are supposed to start acknowledging the occasion.

Choose a strong one
  when using bows,
Take the long ones
  when choosing arrows;
To shoot people,
  first fell their steeds,
To nab bandits,
  catch the one who leads.
    —*Tang dynasty poet Du Fu*

STRATAGEM

18 撶賊撶王

Qin zei qin wang

Catch the ringleader to nab the bandits

THE ASSUMPTION behind this stratagem is that a body deprived of its head cannot function. This principle was ritualized in an early form of Chinese warfare before the invention of firearms, when two opposing commanders would fight it out on horseback in an open space while their troops stood in formation on the sidelines and watched. When one commander lost, his troops would flee and the winning side would pursue to kill.

The stratagem also suggests the more general principle that a force will dissipate when whatever holds it together—be it organization, charisma, or glue—is lost. As a Chinese saying goes, "When the tree falls, the monkeys scatter."

Zhang Xun, a Tang dynasty general sent to defend the

strategic city of Suiyang from insurgents in A.D. 757, knew the importance of catching the ringleader to nab the bandits. After twenty days under siege by the rebels, Suiyang was in such desperate straits that Zhang Xun ordered his concubine to commit suicide and then cooked her to feed his soldiers. Finally one night he and his troops burst out of the city gate on horseback, killed more than 5,000 rebels, including fifty officers, and threw the rebel camp into confusion. In the chaos Zhang Xun wanted to kill the rebel commander, Yin Ziqi, but didn't know who or where he was.

Zhang Xun identified the rebel chief in a clever way: he told his men to use wormwood branches for arrows. Seeing this pitiful ammunition, the rebels concluded that Zhang Xun had run out of arrows. Many rebel soldiers picked up the branches and rushed to report the matter to their leader, hoping to get a reward for breaking the good news. Zhang Xun thus identified Yin Ziqi, and an aide shot an arrow into his left eye. Yin Ziqi fled in pain and the siege collapsed. Over the next few years the entire rebellion was suppressed, and Tang dynasty rule continued for another century and a half.

Because leaders hold such influence over the behavior of those beneath them, assassination has been a favorite tactic in military and political struggles throughout history. Small wonder that Chiang Kai-shek's own generals kidnapped him when they wanted to turn the Kuomintang against the Japanese. Not surprising that Mao Zedong had an exorbitant price on his head during his civil war with Chiang. Not surprising either that the Central Intelligence Agency considered assassinating Fidel Castro by poisoning his cigar or mining his scuba-diving grounds.

The television networks know the power of their stars. In line with their power to draw audience ratings, the likes of Dan Rather, Barbara Walters, and Connie Chung are competed for and handsomely rewarded because, as their titles suggest, they anchor not only individual newscasts or programs but entire news divisions.

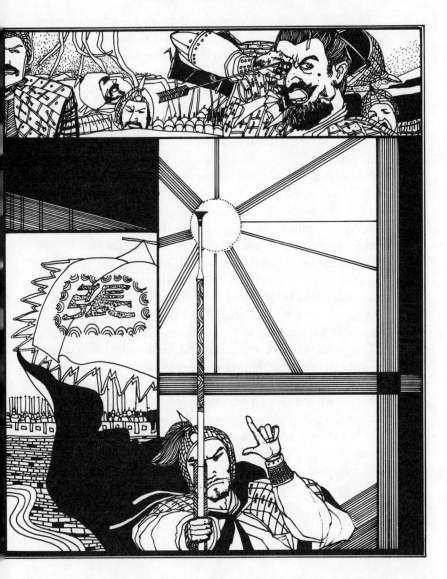

The clever Zhang Xun, knowing he has to "catch the ringleader to nab the bandits," uses a ruse to identify the rebel chief Yin Ziqi and then has an aide shoot an arrow into the chieftain's eye, whereupon the insurgent troops are thrown into confusion and the rebellion collapses.

The absence of a leader opens the way for adversaries to mount an attack or consolidate a defense. Henry Ford waited until Iacocca was traveling in the Mideast on a *Time* magazine junket to sabotage his position at Ford. On the eve of a trip to China, John Sculley learned that Steve Jobs was lobbying the board of directors of Apple in an effort to retain his operations management position. Sculley, who had been trying to ease Jobs out of that position, cancelled the trip.

Businesses often ignore powerful adversarial movements at their peril. But the clever ones have discovered that it is possible to co-opt adversaries without giving up a great deal. A company can gain legitimacy and credibility by merely giving labor leaders or consumer advocates an ear. When Chrysler received a multibillion-dollar bailout from the federal government in 1979, it also accepted a reform plan that included inviting United Auto Workers president Douglas Fraser to join the board of directors. This move was vital for securing political support for the bailout.

The stratagem of catching the ringleader to nab the bandits points out the value of decentralized systems of administration. When everything depends on the leader, achievements hinge on his effectiveness, and his absence is acutely felt. But if responsibility is shared, the talents of others will be freer to emerge, and the entity won't collapse if the leader departs. This principle operates in families and informal groups as well as in corporations, government, and other formal institutions. If all the housework depends on Mom, it's no wonder the household falls apart when she gets sick.

FOUR

STRATAGEMS FOR CONFUSED SITUATIONS

Disorderly or chaotic circumstances involving various contending forces call for a complex juggling of interests and relationships. Stratagems in this set recognize that alliances based on short-term interest may be required to cope with an opponent, while alliances among adversaries may have to be broken. They employ such techniques as negotiation and peace overtures mingled with threats, manipulation of third parties, and divisive ploys.

> *To get rid of weeds, dig up the roots; to stop a pot from boiling, withdraw the fuel.*
> —CHINESE PROVERB

STRATAGEM

19

Fu di chou xin

Steal the firewood from under the cauldron

THIS STRATAGEM comes in handy when your opponent has the edge. Rather than resisting him directly, this method aims at depleting his resources and sapping his spirit.

In the spring of A.D. 200 at the Battle of Guandu—an event often cited by Mao to encourage his peasant army in the face of a much stronger opponent—Cao Cao's army of 20,000 used the stratagem of stealing firewood from under the cauldron to wipe out Yuan Shao's force of 100,000.

Yuan Shao was a warlord ruling over the vast area north of the Yellow River. Cao Cao, at the time the power behind the throne of the declining Eastern Han dynasty, controlled a smaller territory to the south between the Yellow River and the Yangtze. When Yuan Shao was preparing to cross the Yellow River and attack Cao Cao at Guandu, his advisers suggested he wait for Cao Cao to run out of supplies, knowing that the troops on the other side were well trained but short on grain and fodder. The impatient Yuan Shao ignored the advice and crossed the river anyway.

Several months of skirmishing ensued. When Yuan Shao besieged Cao Cao's camp and built earthen mounds around it to shoot arrows from, Cao Cao's men built rock catapults to destroy the mounds. When Yuan Shao's troops tried to approach the camp by digging tunnels, Cao Cao countered by having a deep trench dug around the camp. Meanwhile Cao Cao's army was running out of food. The officer in charge of grain suggested using smaller measuring vessels, and Cao Cao agreed, but his soldiers began to complain. So Cao Cao had the officer beheaded and displayed the head on a flagpole for all his men to see. He said the officer had been embezzling grain, and for a time the soldiers were appeased.

In this critical situation, Cao Cao sent a message to his base calling for more grain supplies. The message was intercepted by an adviser to Yuan Shao named Xu You who happened to be an old childhood friend of Cao Cao's. As a result of a dispute with Yuan Shao, Xu You decided to defect to Cao Cao's side. He let himself be captured by Cao Cao's sentries. Cao Cao emerged from his tent in his pajamas to greet his old friend.

Xu You convinced Cao Cao that the answer to his predicament was not to seek more supplies to be able to continue fighting Yuan Shao head-on, but to destroy Yuan Shao's storehouses. Disguising a detachment of soldiers with uniforms and banners like Yuan Shao's, Cao Cao led them to Yuan Shao's logistics center. They moved under cover of night, the soldiers clenching chopsticks in their teeth so they would not talk, accompanied by muzzled horses. The commander in charge of guarding the base, a chronic drunkard, was fast asleep. Cao Cao's men burned the storehouses to the ground. Cao Cao also ordered the noses chopped off the enemy commander and soldiers before releasing them to report to Yuan Shao.

On the principle of "stealing the firewood from under the cauldron," Cao Cao seeks to deprive his enemy of both physical and mental sustenance; he sends his troops to burn down Yuan Shao's store-houses, thus destroying their grain, and also has his troops chop off enemy soldiers' noses, thus destroying their morale.

At the sight of the billowing smoke and flames sent up by the inferno and then the arrival of the mutilated commander and his men, the rest of Yuan Shao's army was struck with fear and scattered in disarray. When Cao Cao returned to attack them, only a few hundred mounted troops were able to follow Yuan Shao across the Yellow River and flee north.

This story illustrates that withdrawing firewood has a double meaning—one can deprive the enemy of physical sustenance, in this case grain, and also of psychological sustenance, here confidence and morale.

Knocking out physical support is as important as ever in warfare—for instance, in its actions at Midway Island in World War II, the U.S. navy sank four Japanese aircraft carriers so that enemy fighter planes had no place to land; and in the Iran-Iraq war, each side attacked the other's oil fields and petrochemical refineries to cripple the economy.

But eliminating the enemy's psychological support system may be even more important. Napoleon once observed that three-quarters of an army's strength consists of morale. Many ancient commanders were well aware of this. When Liu Bang, founder of the Han dynasty, and Xiang Yu, head of the kingdom of Chu, were struggling over the rule of China in 202 B.C., Liu Bang's soldiers were ordered to sing Chu folksongs every night, making their opponents so homesick that they could not fight and suffered disastrous defeat. Two hundred years later during the Jin dynasty, when a minority tribe besieged a city in a border region, commander Liu Kun climbed the city wall three nights in a row and sat under the stars playing mournful tribal tunes on a reed pipe. The tribesmen, moved to tears, withdrew without a fight.

One of the principles Mao formulated for his peasant army was "Break down the enemy forces by political work." In combination with military methods, the technique proved so successful that by the eve of the Communist victory in 1949, whole divisions of Chiang Kai-shek's troops were defecting to the other side.

Business provides many examples of removal or expropriation of underlying support systems. When a corporate raider begins quietly buying up stock in a targeted company, in essence he is stealing firewood until he acquires enough to assert control.

An Indiana company trying to defend itself against a raider used the strategy of stealing firewood in a different way. When Canada's Belzberg family expressed an interest in the Indiana-based auto-parts giant Arvin Industries in late 1985, the chairman of Arvin invited a friend to lunch. The friend was president of the state senate. By the time the Belzbergs were ready to tender an offer, a bill that in effect outlawed most hostile takeovers in the state had been steered through the Indiana legislature and onto the governor's desk, where it was promptly signed. The Belzbergs had to back off because the firewood under the cauldron— that is, a permissive legal environment—had been removed.

A type of firewood that is vital to the financial health of computer producers is computer operating systems. IBM made MS-DOS the most prevalent operating system for personal computers, with the once-popular CP/M now nearly defunct. And in the minicomputer field, IBM, DEC, and a few other companies have been contending with Sun Microsystems, which is allied with more than a score of other firms, over what the standard version of the Unix operating system should be. Whichever side ends up with the winning system will have a big advantage, because software makers will produce software for the standard system and customers will naturally want the system for which the most applications are available.

Large companies trying to hedge their bets with smaller competitors may try to extend control over basic systems early on. This is evident in anticipatory dealings involving Next Inc., a company founded by former Apple Computer chairman Steve Jobs, that is yet to prove itself commercially viable. In 1988 IBM paid more than $10 million to license the Nextstep technology, a set of advanced software tools that simplify the design of computer programs. And the Japanese electronics firm Canon invested $100 million in Next in return for the right to market Next computers in Asia.

U.S. business might make more headway in cracking the Japanese market if Americans understood the nature of the firewood under the cauldron of the Japanese system. U.S. interests are hampered not so much by overt tariffs and quotas but more by nontariff barriers—Japan's byzantine import regulations, complex distribution system, and impenetrable web of business relationships.

The stratagem of stealing the firewood from under the cauldron should remind us that business relations, friendship, and love rest on complex support systems that must be tended and maintained. If a basic prop gives way—for instance, if a trust is betrayed—an important relationship can collapse. On the other hand, if you can continue to stoke the fires beneath the relationship—don't stop paying college tuition for your son or daughter just because you aren't talking to each other—superficial ruptures can be mended later on.

STRATAGEM

20 混水摸魚

Hun shui mo yu

Fish in troubled waters

THE PRINCIPLE of this stratagem is that inopportune times provide unusual opportunities. In confusing or chaotic circumstances, people lose their sense of orientation and have a hard time telling the spurious from the genuine and the good from the bad. A bank robber who strikes during a blackout or looters who rampage through stores after a hurricane are unlikely to be caught.

This stratagem is reminiscent of Stratagem 5, looting a burning house, in that both take advantage of misfortune. In either case, one might make the most of misfortunes that already exist, or seek to benefit from deliberately created misfortunes. However, the types of misfortunes are different: looting a burning house refers to taking advantage of an opponent's particular adversities, while fishing in troubled waters means taking advantage of a general situation of confusion and chaos.

Troubled situations create possibilities for different interests to win over the middle, swallow the weak, and destabilize the strong. Ambitious people throughout Chinese history have recognized this; time and again, contending forces have emerged to take advantage of political confusion, economic breakdown, and social disarray in periods of war, famine, or the disintegration of a dynasty. The chronicles of the Three Kingdoms period are nothing but a tale of numerous players playing the game of fishing in troubled waters.

Perhaps the greatest achievement ever made by fishing in troubled waters was Liu Bei's establishment of one of those famed Three Kingdoms, the kingdom of Shu. Liu Bei took advantage of a climate of chaos that prevailed after the defeat of strongman Cao Cao at the Battle of Red Cliff to take the city of Jinzhou at a strategic spot on the Yangtze River. He then took advantage of internal struggles faced by a warlord in another city, Yizhou, and established his base there.

Sun Zi was thinking of more active employment of this stratagem when he advised, "Force the enemy into a state of chaos and then crush him." Goujian, the king of Yue, followed this active approach in 496 B.C. when he led his troops to fend off an attack by the kingdom of Wu. As the two armies faced each other, three columns among the Yue ranks suddenly pulled out their swords and slashed their own throats. So shocked were the Wu attackers that they scrambled in all directions, some to run away, others to get a closer look. At this moment, Goujian counterattacked and defeated the Wu. In fact, Goujian had orchestrated this drama at little cost: the kamikaze soldiers actually were condemned prisoners who had been given the choice of execution or suicide and had chosen the latter.

Throughout human history, fishing in troubled waters has brought on everything from revolutions in social organization to breakthroughs in our knowledge about the world.

Political revolutions occur in large part because they represent an alternative to systems with which people have grown weary, or disgusted, or outraged. The Bolsheviks came to victory on the corruption and inefficiency of decaying tsarist Russia. After a vast, ill-equipped, and unprepared conscript army had been sent into the cauldron of World War I, the revolutionaries seized power amid war-weariness, food riots, and mutinies and signed a separate peace with Germany. The Chinese Revolution triumphed after nearly a century of constant warfare. The populace, disillusioned with the corruption and brutality of the Kuomintang regime and burdened by galloping inflation and other economic problems, welcomed the Communist victory with high hopes in 1949.

In his classic book *The Structure of Scientific Revolutions*, Thomas Kuhn observes that major advances in scientific inquiry have always entailed great upheaval, causing fundamental realignment of entire disciplines and fields. His idea of "paradigm shift" has been extended to the social sciences and humanities as well. From this perspective, fishing in troubled waters is to be valued as an engine of progress.

One can make a parallel argument for business, where the emergence of new technologies, the realignment of an industry, or the reorganization of a company provide opportunities for entrepreneurs and managers to achieve, to score, and to advance. Turmoil is what injects the electronics industry, biotechnology, and other growing fields with dynamism and excitement, and spurs the search for ever-superior products and techniques. Management guru Tom Peters recognizes the value of upheaval in opening up new paths for individuals, organizations, and industries—he made it the theme of an entire book, *Thriving on Chaos*.

Business also yields some crass examples of fishing in troubled waters—such as the merchants who profited from brisk sales of T-shirts and sweatshirts announcing "I survived the quake of 1989!" after the catastrophe in San Francisco. But such is to be expected in a competitive environment.

There is little to be gained by fishing in troubled waters in personal relationships. When the water is clear and placid, you can see well enough to evaluate others and they in turn can assess you clearly. You should be on your guard against people who want to make friends when muddy water obscures their motives as well as your view of them.

> *Misleading the enemy by false*
> *appearance—this is what strategy*
> *is all about.*
>
> *—100 WAYS OF WARRING*
> *(BAIZHAN QILUE)*

STRATAGEM

21 金蝉悦壳

Jin chan tuo qiao

Slough off the cicada's shell

IF YOU EVER TRIED to fool your mother into thinking you were in bed when you weren't by stuffing pillows under the blanket then you understand this stratagem. It means to create the impression of remaining in one place while you move to a different place from which you can launch a sneak attack.

Sloughing off the cicada's shell plays on the yin-yang relationship between presence and absence, form and content, withdrawal and advance. It is reflected in the *Book of Changes* hexagram number 18, meaning decay or destruction, with the implication that things going to ruin can be restored to soundness and vigor.

Lu Bu, an awesome fighter of the second century B.C., used this stratagem to save his own life. Lu Bu had lent

An aide pretends to be commander Lu Bu playing the zither, while Lu Bu himself slips out of his tent to safety; enemy soldiers who come to kill him that night merely chop up the quilt he's left lumped in his bed—he has "sloughed off the cicada's shell."

his services to Yuan Shao, who then controlled a large part of North China. But even after Lu Bu had helped to put down a peasant rebellion, Yuan Shao was suspicious and afraid of him and asked him to leave, which Lu Bu agreed to do. On further thought, Yuan Shao worried that he was merely "returning a tiger to the mountains" and decided to kill Lu Bu.

When Lu Bu departed, Yuan Shao sent thirty warriors along with him, saying they were for his protection—but in fact the soldiers had orders to kill Lu Bu. That night they camped around Lu Bu's tent. When it got dark, Lu Bu, who was known as a good zither player, asked a trusted aide to play the zither while he slipped out. The soldiers thought Lu Bu was still in his tent and waited for the zither playing to stop so they could kill him in his sleep. Finally the music ceased, and some time later the soldiers ran into the tent and chopped up the sleeping form they assumed was Lu Bu.

The next morning Yuan Shao's people were astonished to find that Lu Bu's troops had gone, and that the body they thought they had chopped up was nothing but a cotton quilt.

An extension of this stratagem is creating a false impression to deflect an attack onto others. This is how the kingdom of Chu once preserved itself from harm during the Warring States period.

At the time, the kingdom of Qin was poised to conquer the other six kingdoms, and it looked as though the kingdom of Han would go first. So the king of Han began negotiating a deal with Qin to make Qin attack the much richer Chu first. The price for Han would be concession of a city and some weaponry.

When the news reached the king of Chu, he declared that he was going to Han's rescue and sent an emissary to inform the king of Han that Chu would wholeheartedly defend that kingdom. He then ordered his troops to march toward Han in a great display. The king of Han was happy with this new development and called off negotiations with Qin.

The king of Qin was enraged and attacked Han. Qin eventually conquered a major city of Han, and the king of Han had to send his own son to Qin as a hostage during peace negotiations. The kingdom of Chu came out unscathed.

Sloughing off the cicada's shell appears in diplomacy whenever a nation threatened by another tries to give the impression of compliance. Stalin's secret agreement with Hitler before World War II was a gesture of accommodation intended to prevent an assault on the Soviet Union. Although the Germans still invaded, some argue that the pact at least bought time. Similarly, the Munich Pact was an attempt by France and Britain to forestall German invasion with a display of accommodation—which also did not work very long.

Businesses sometimes use the cicada shell stratagem to divert attention from one place to another. Some believe the main purpose of hiring strategy consultants is as a lightning rod to draw criticism away from the CEO. The consultant comes in, listens to what the CEO wants to do, and writes it down. Management can then present this "objective" report by an outsider to bolster its case before the board of directors, the stockholders, and the public.

Firms that are in difficulty or under criticism sometimes reshuffle top management to present a new face—hoping that the cicada shells of new officers will restore confidence even if true power resides elsewhere. In an effort to bolster prospects for the world's largest advertising agency, Saatchi & Saatchi, after two years of scattershot acquisitions and financial problems, cofounder Maurice Saatchi relinquished the post of chief executive to a barely known French executive and named an even lesser-known Frenchman chief financial officer. Some praised the surprising appointments, but one critic likened them to "rearranging the deck chairs on the *Titanic*," and others doubted the new officers could survive the office politics that had plagued others in the company's higher echelons before.

In some circumstances, the cicada's shell is a liability that a company truly wants to abandon. Christie Hefner, having taken over the Playboy empire from her father Hugh, is trying to shed the frolicking Playboy reputation of the past in favor of a more sophisticated, businesslike image.

Creating illusions in your working and personal life may be necessary from time to time for tactical reasons. A simple example is calling in sick from work when you aren't in order to take care of some matter that may or may not be urgent. But sloughing off the cicada's shell should not be done too often. Illusions are hard to maintain, and if you are found out just once, others may decide you are not to be trusted ever.

> *One desperado on the run can*
> *scare off one thousand men.*
> —*Warring States Strategist Wu Qi*

STRATAGEM

22 閧凶捉贼

Guan men zhuo zei

Shut the door to catch the thief

THE NAME of the Red River in North China's Shanxi province is a reminder of a battle that took place more than two thousand years ago, when the water coursed red with the blood of 400,000 soldiers. The bloodshed resulted from the cruelest example in Chinese history of shutting the door to catch the thief. The strategist responsible for this outcome was the famed commander Bai Qi of the state of Qin, which gained ascendancy during the Warring States period. Bai Qi shut the door not once, but twice—first to achieve a military victory, and second to massacre his hapless adversaries.

The story begins in 262 B.C. when Qin sent an expeditionary army against the territory of Shangdang, belonging to the weaker state of Han. The governor of Shangdang

128

responded by turning over the seventeen cities under his control to the state of Zhao, anticipating that Qin would redirect its wrath toward Zhao and then Zhao would have to ally itself with Han to expel the Qin invaders.

Zhao sent an army of 200,000 men under the command of Lian Po to defend Shangdang. By the time they arrived, Shangdang had already fallen to the Qin. Lian Po encamped his troops near the banks of the Red River, where they built fortifications and dug deep water-storage pits. This enabled them to withstand Qin troops for nearly three years.

In 260 B.C. Qin's mastermind military strategist Fan Ju decided to put an end to the standoff. Using the strategy of sowing discord among the enemy (see Stratagem 33), he bribed people in the capital of Zhao to spread rumors against Lian Po. He also put out a rumor saying the Qin army most feared that Zhao Kuo, son of a recently deceased marshal, would be sent as the new commander.

Before his death, Zhao Kuo's father had felt a premonition that Zhao Kuo would bring disaster upon the state of Zhao if he were allowed to command troops. On his deathbed, the marshal had told his wife that if the king of Zhao wanted Zhao Kuo to lead troops, she should advise against it. But when that time came, the king ignored her pleas. Falling right into the Qin trap, he named Zhao Kuo to replace Lian Po. Zhao Kuo brought another 200,000 troops, making a total force of 400,000. Meanwhile, Qin secretly sent to the front the famous Bai Qi.

Unlike Lian Po, Zhao Kuo responded to Qin provocations. When he won his first battle by pitting 10,000 of his men against 3,000 sent by the Qin, he was so elated with victory that he challenged the Qin army to a decisive fight the next day. Bai Qi's deputy agreed, and then Bai Qi ordered his army to pull back, which Zhao Kuo took as a sign of fear.

The next day two Qin generals led 10,000 troops each to battle the Zhao army and deliberately let Zhao Kuo win in order to lure him out farther. Meanwhile two more generals, each with 15,000 men, circled around to the rear of the Zhao army to cut off its supply lines. Once the Zhao soldiers had emerged from their fortifications, another Qin general with 20,000 men cut the Zhao force in two. Two more Qin generals leading 5,000 cavalry troops each stood by ready to decimate the Zhao army. Furthermore, when Zhao Kuo sent messengers home to ask for reinforcements, the king of Qin conscripted every Qin male over the age of fourteen who was not yet in the army and personally led them to the front.

For forty-six days Zhao Kuo's troops were completely cut off from supplies and assistance. His starving soldiers began to kill one another for food. In desperation, Zhao Kuo tried to break out of the encirclement with a shock force of 5,000 men. Zhao Kuo and all his men were killed, and the remaining Zhao troops surrendered.

But Bai Qi did not stop there. He divided the Zhao soldiers into ten camps, each with 40,000 Zhao soldiers and 20,000 Qin soldiers. The Zhao soldiers were wined and dined and told that the next day a select group would be drafted into the Qin army and the rest could go home. Overjoyed, they went to sleep. Meanwhile, all Qin soldiers were instructed to wrap white cloths around their heads at midnight. Anyone without such a cloth was to be killed. The Zhao soldiers all had their heads chopped off in their sleep. The only survivors were 240 teenagers whom Bai Qi spared so they could go home to report the bad news. Within a few years the entire kingdom of Zhao had fallen to the Qin.

The stratagem of shutting the door to catch the thief— in essence, encircling the enemy and closing off all escape routes—has some important prerequisites. First, in order to shut the door, one must have at least a locally superior concentration of forces if not absolute superiority. Sun Zi indicated this when he wrote, "If our force is ten times that of the enemy, we'll encircle it; five times, attack it; and twice, divide it." Second, there must be a house with a door to shut—namely, some sort of trap, be it physical or psychological. Third, one cannot wait passively for the thief to enter the house; often, he must be lured. Fourth, one must close the door at the proper time so that the thief is truly shut in.

Fifth, the windows and any other possible outlet must be shut off, too. "Cornered beasts will still fight," a Chinese saying observes. If the thief perceives any possibility of escape, he will fight desperately. But if he knows fighting is hopeless, he will give up. The encirclement must be as ironclad as Bai Qi's.

Mao Zedong was cognizant of these requirements when he ordered the city of Jinzhou taken at the start of the campaign to capture China's northeast during the civil war. Jinzhou was the bottleneck linking Manchuria with the rest of China. Once this city was in Communist hands, the Kuomintang armies in the northeast could neither escape nor obtain reinforcements. Half a million Kuomintang troops perished in the battle that followed the taking of Jinzhou.

In business, shutting the door to catch the thief may be applied by a strong company wishing to overpower a fledgling challenger. If an established firm anticipates intense competition over a new product, for instance, it may want to adjust its pricing policy accordingly. Instead of pricing high in the early stages of the product's life cycle—a common method for capturing those customers for whom the product has the greatest value and who will pay the most—the company may want to preempt the competition's strategy by penetration pricing or pricing the product low to set up entry barriers while increasing volume, cutting down production costs, and taking advantage of economies of scale.

In Silicon Valley, big companies sometimes attempt to stymie small start-ups with patent-encroachment lawsuits. The small companies are choked to death with legal expenses.

The stratagem of shutting the door to catch the thief is an obvious technique to use when negotiating for a raise or promotion. You back your employer into a corner—

either he concedes or you leave. To do this, however, you must be in an advantageous position. Preferably, you are valued in your present job and have another lucrative job offer lined up. You cannot bluff with this stratagem because you need an alternative in case you miscalculate and your boss turns you down.

Shutting the door to catch the thief is a dangerous stratagem to use in personal relationships precisely because it leaves the other party with no escape, and does not allow you to backtrack either. It may be most useful in implementing a hard decision to end a relationship—a decision which itself should never be taken without much thought and consideration of other routes. If a partner in a long-term arrangement finally decides the situation cannot be salvaged, the least painful solution may be a swift ultimatum to end it. Preparation must be as tight as a drum: if fighting over children is anticipated, measures for protecting them from psychological or physical harm should be worked out first. If fighting over finances is expected, one should figure out how far one wants to go to maintain one's share of the spoils, and lawyers should be lined up. But this is an extreme situation, and for most ordinary purposes one seldom needs to resort to shutting the door.

People with different dreams
can share the same bed.
                    —CHINESE SAYING

STRATAGEM

23 遠交近攻

Yuan jiao jin gong

Befriend a distant state while
attacking a neighbor

THIS STRATAGEM plays on the yin-yang relationship between friends and enemies, near and far, and concentration
versus dispersion. Its application revolves around the problems posed by geographical constraints. Under most circumstances, striking at an objective close to home is
preferable to making a long journey to reach a distant target. If one befriends distant enemies while attacking nearby
ones, one can minimize logistical difficulties and consolidate each victory in turn.

These tactical friendships are based on the principle that
even people as different as fire and water can sometimes
side together for a common benefit. This idea is reflected
in the *Book of Changes* hexagram number 38, which means
separation. This symbol denotes a social state in which

division prevails, but it also suggests that in small matters, this condition can be healed. In other words, even in disunion one can discover friends.

The stratagem of befriending a distant state while attacking a neighbor is credited to Fan Ju, prime minister of the kingdom of Qin, who helped establish China's first unified empire. Qin was the strongest of seven contenders during the Warring States period, a period characterized by constant contention among neighbors—"swallowing like whales and nibbling like silkworms," as the saying goes. Alliances were many and shifting as each kingdom strove for its own advantage. Finally in 332 B.C. the kingdoms of Qi, Chu, Yan, Han, Zhao, and Wei signed a formal treaty to align against Qin. At a ceremony the kings of the six weaker kingdoms painted their lips with animal blood and vowed to abide by the treaty. The pact was basically maintained for many years—until 265 B.C., when Fan Ju became Qin's prime minister in a most unusual rise to power.

Fan Ju's career had begun in his native Wei, where he worked for an official named Xu Jia. On a diplomatic trip Fan Ju impressed the king of Qi and was invited to stay, but declined. However, he did accept gifts of gold, meat, and wine. Xu Jia reported this to the prime minister of Wei, Wei Qi, who had Fan Ju tortured and thrown into a latrine where he was left for dead. But a sympathetic guard rescued him, and he changed his name and went into hiding in the mountains. Half a year later, he disguised himself as a servant at a hotel where a Qin diplomat was staying and so impressed the diplomat with his knowledge of geopolitics that the diplomat took him to Qin and recommended him for an official position.

At the time Qin's prime minister was Duke Rang, the brother of the Qin king's mother. Duke Rang jealously guarded his access to the king. A year passed, and Fan Ju still had not been considered for a position. Finally he wrote a letter requesting an audience with the king about plans laid by Duke Rang to attack the kingdom of Qi. The king summoned Fan Ju and listened to his analysis.

Fan Ju said Qi was too far away from Qin and further-more separated from it by Han and Wei. If Qin sent a small army, it would be unable to defeat Qi and would only suffer humiliation. If Qin sent a large army, it would be wasting resources to help Han and Wei. A better approach, Fan Ju recommended, was to befriend two distant states, Qi and Chu, and attack those nearby, Han and Wei. The king im-mediately cancelled the plan to attack Qi and named Fan Ju his senior security adviser.

As the king's trust in Fan Ju grew, Fan Ju warned him that his mother and uncle had usurped too much power. The king immediately dismissed Duke Rang, put the em-press dowager under house arrest, and named Fan Ju prime minister. Fan Ju's first target was the kingdom that had subjected him to so much humiliation—his own birthplace of Wei.

Wei tried to forestall the attack by attempting to bribe the new prime minister. The official entrusted with the task was the very official who had betrayed Fan Ju, Xu Jia. Upon seeing the man who reportedly had expired in a latrine, Xu Jia fell to his knees and begged for forgiveness. Fan Ju could have killed him but merely humiliated him by in-viting him to a banquet and serving him nothing but boiled black beans which he had to eat like a horse from the hands of two criminals. Then he sent Xu Jia back to Wei with the message that Qin would attack unless Wei delivered the head of its prime minister, Wei Qi. At the news, Wei Qi killed himself. His head was sent to Fan Ju, who had it dried, lacquered, and made into a chamber pot.

Qin proceeded to follow Fan Ju's prescription, making peace with the distant Qi and Chu and attacking the nearby Han. The six-state alliance quickly fell apart. Qin swal-lowed Han first, Zhao next (as related in Stratagem 22), and then Wei, Chu, Yan, and finally Qi.

The difficulties of achieving and consolidating victory over distant lands is illustrated by the history of coloni-alism. Once the sun never set on the British Empire; but in time, Britain found it impossible to hold on to all its distant colonies. The experience of the United States in Korea and Vietnam also shows this. Tsarist Russia, on the other hand, expanded eastward and swallowed about 1.5 million square kilometers of Chinese territory, most of which Moscow still claims. And Israel relies on its backing by a distant superpower, the United States, as well as co-existence with Arab countries lying some distance from it such as Saudi Arabia and Kuwait, while fighting in neigh-boring Lebanon and maintaining a firm grip on the West Bank and Gaza Strip.

Of course, befriending in this stratagem does not mean perpetual peace. As a saying goes, "There are permanent interests, not permanent friends." The United States and Japan, once enemies, are now allies. The United States and the USSR, former allies, seem to be making peace again after four decades of Cold War antagonism. Enmity be-tween nations may last as long as one or the other—or neither—prevails; but unfortunately, one cannot count on these friendships lasting forever either.

The implications for business are clear: a company should make alliances for a common interest and should not take on too many challenges at once. In launching a new product, a firm should work in familiar territory and then roll out. Companies should avoid overdiversification, which is tantamount to attacking distant lands.

The keen competition in the computer industry has forced companies into all sorts of alliances. AT&T and Sun Microsystems joined forces to establish a new software standard, developing a system merging the most popular versions of the Unix operating system into a single product with the backing of an eighteen-member industry consor-tium. Arrayed against them was another consortium in-cluding Hewlett-Packard, Digital, and IBM, which proved slower in coming up with its competing version of Unix and grew increasingly conciliatory as the AT&T group neared success.

Another pact was formed between Microsoft Corporation and Apple Computer, rivals that had fought in court over printer technology for many years. In the fall of 1989, the two companies announced they had reached agreement on sharing on-line font technology and printer software. The loser in this truce was Adobe, maker of software and typefonts that until that point were the favored standard for high-end desktop publishing systems. According to some analysts, if Adobe had compromised on licensing with the two more powerful firms a year earlier, a power struggle would have been avoided and Adobe could have become the unified standard.

Players in the automobile industry have used this strategy internationally, as witnessed by the joint ventures between General Motors and Toyota, Ford and Nissan, and Chrysler and Mitsubishi. In fact, it is interesting that even as Japan-bashing has intensified in Washington, individual states have pursued their own policies of courting Japan. Up to thirty-seven states have offices in Tokyo, and by the late 1990s Japan is expected to overtake Britain as the largest foreign investor in the United States.

Individuals in an organization can also make use of befriending a distant state. Whether you want to move up in the organization, consolidate support for a controversial proposal, or undermine an idea you think is bad, there almost always will be others blocking your way. To achieve your goal, you should never make too many enemies, and if you have to have some, choose them carefully: take on the weakest first and, if possible, take on just one at a time.

Tactical alliances are not only useful but virtually mandatory in personal and family life. To maintain your friendships, you have to at least try to get along with your friends' friends. To maintain peace in the family, you have to develop a modus vivendi with your relatives' relatives. These are relationships not of choice but of necessity.

Occasionally, befriending a distant state may mean becoming an accomplice in a cause you dislike for the sake of a more important goal. For instance, if your child likes junk food and fast driving, you're wiser to accept the former preference at least tactically while concentrating on opposing the more immediate danger of car accidents, the leading cause of death among American teenagers.

Without the lips, the teeth will be cold.

—CHINESE IDIOM

STRATAGEM

24 假道伐虢

Jia dao fa guo

Obtain safe passage to conquer the kingdom of Guo

THE STRATAGEM of obtaining safe passage is appropriate when one of your adversaries is threatened by another. If you intervene on behalf of the first adversary, you can extend your influence over both adversaries at the same time. This idea is reflected in the *Book of Changes* hexagram number 47, meaning predicament, which implies that when someone else is in peril, you can't win his trust by empty words alone—action, not mere talk, is required.

This stratagem plays on the yin-yang relationship between borrowing and lending, regularity and surprise, concentration and division, and forming and breaking alliances. An early example dates from the Spring and Autumn period some 2,500 years ago when the lords of fiefdoms granted by the Eastern Zhou court were vying to expand their territories. Among the fiefdoms were two small kingdoms in the north called Yu and Guo. Both bordered on the much larger kingdom of Jin that wanted to swallow them up but could not as long as the two got along.

In 658 B.C. a Jin official came up with the idea of attacking Guo via Yu. First, Jin border guards provoked skirmishes on the border with Guo. Then Jin presented the king of Yu with two treasures, a horse and a piece of jade, to entice him into allowing Jin troops passage to Xiyang Pass on the Yu-Guo border. Despite an adviser's warning that the only thing protecting Yu and Guo was their cooperation, the Yu king agreed. Furthermore, the Yu king fooled the general guarding Guo's side of the pass by saying he was sending some chariots across to help Guo fight some minority tribes. In fact they were Jin chariots, and Jin soldiers jumped out and took the pass by surprise. The Jin troops besieged the Guo capital for four months until the king of Guo finally fled with a handful of supporters. Then Jin easily took over Guo.

Jin rewarded the king of Yu with one-third of the booty seized from Guo. Meanwhile Jin's top general pretended to fall ill, and the Yu ruler sent doctors to attend to him. While the general faked his recuperation, the king of Jin paid a visit to Yu. The king of Yu took the king of Jin to a hunting competition and, wanting to impress his more powerful neighbor, brought along his best soldiers, chariots, and horses. While the king of Yu was preoccupied with showing off this way, the Jin general arose from his phony sickbed and captured the Yu capital.

The key to this stratagem is the ability to borrow a passage. During the Vietnam War, the United States relied on borrowed territory—its airbases in Thailand and the Philippines—to get men, matériel, and bombs to Vietnam. And the North Vietnamese borrowed border regions in Cambodia to avoid U.S. saturation bombing—and later took not only South Vietnam but also Cambodia. In the Reagan era, the United States positioned itself against Sandinista Nicaragua not only in rhetoric but also by beefing up its military presence in Honduras, and if not for public sentiment against another Vietnam might well have launched an invasion of Nicaragua from there.

The classic version of obtaining safe passage to conquer the kingdom of Guo involves a stronger party making use of a weaker one. A variation of the strategy is when the weak one uses the strong one's resources to build itself up and then comes back to swallow up the strong one. Japan and West Germany, defeated in World War II, have become major economic competitors of the United States after rebuilding with U.S. economic aid. Microsoft Corporation gained a dominant status among software manufacturers by riding on IBM's success, and now not only IBM but untold numbers of other personal computer manufacturers rely on its MS-DOS operating system as an industry standard. Charles Wang's Computer Associates International, which began with four employees in 1976 as a subsidiary of a Swiss software company, went on to devour its parent and acquire nearly a score of other software houses, becoming the world's largest independent software company.

At work, this stratagem may prove useful when you are developing a project that you or your office cannot accomplish alone. It is important to cultivate good relations with everyone from members of the secretarial pool and the mailroom staff to the legal counsel and those in the executive suites—not only to make going to work a pleasurable social activity, but also because obtaining safe passage through other offices and divisions may be the only way to reach the help or resources that you require to get jobs done.

If you would like to make a mark in professional or political circles or other community causes, this stratagem suggests that getting involved in a small way is a good way to start. Almost everyone who ever became president of an academic organization began by joining committees. Those who are prominent in Democratic or Republican party politics may have started as get-out-the-vote precinct volunteers. Some members of your local school board probably began as agitators in the parent-teacher association. These local-level involvements constitute the safe passage that will lead you on to bigger and better things.

FIVE

STRATAGEMS FOR GAINING GROUND

The underlying aim of this set of stratagems is summed up in the Chinese idiom "Swallowing like a whale and nibbling like a silkworm." One way or another, the intent is to attain what others control. Toward this end, these stratagems make use of replacement techniques, diversionary tactics, misrepresentation, and entrapment.

STRATAGEM

25 偷梁換柱

Tou liang huan zhu

*Replace the beams and pillars
with rotten timber*

To REPLACE a building's sound supports with rotten ones means to steal, sabotage, destroy, or otherwise remove key structures sustaining one's opponent and substitute one's own. In other words, you incapacitate your adversary and gain control from the inside. As hexagram number 63 of the *Book of Changes* notes, "When the wheels are held up, the chariot can't move; when the beams and pillars are withdrawn, the house will fall asunder."

In ancient times military commanders used this stratagem to turn allies into subordinates. Before the age of modern weaponry, battle formation was a crucial element of effective fighting. Troops normally were deployed in a square shape. Down the middle of the formation was the "heavenly balance" or backbone column. Perpendicular to

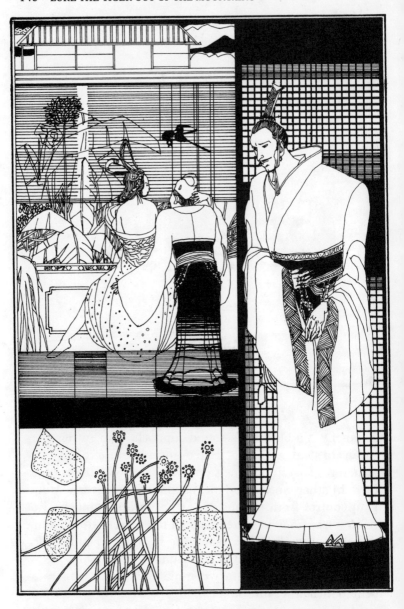

Lu Buwei launches his plan to take over the kingdom of Qin, using the stratagem of "replacing beams and pillars with rotten timbers," by captivating prince Yi Ren with a singsong girl previously impregnated by him.

this column were symmetrical "earth axles." The clever commander could gradually replace the ally's main beams and pillars with his own forces.

Lu Buwei, a wealthy merchant from the state of Zhao during the Warring States period, took over an entire kingdom by supplanting beams and pillars with his own.

In this period of shifting alliances among the seven kingdoms, when two kingdoms signed a treaty one side often required the other to send a royal son or grandson as a guarantor. Yi Ren, grandson of the king of Qin, found himself one such hostage to an alliance between Qin and Zhao. The scheming Lu Buwei, hoping to play on the emotions of a prince far from home, bribed Yi Ren's bodyguards and befriended the lonely and depressed young man. Eventually he parlayed this friendship into control of the Qin throne.

Yi Ren's father was the crown prince, but Yi Ren's mother had long been out of favor. Lu Buwei traveled to Qin and bribed the sister of the king's favorite concubine, Huayang, to curry favor for Yi Ren. The sister talked Huayang into adopting Yi Ren, placing the young man in a good position to inherit the throne.

Returning to Zhao, Lu Buwei purchased a beautiful sing-song girl and impregnated her. Then he invited Yi Ren to dinner, where the woman captivated the young prince with her dancing and singing. Lu Buwei surprised Yi Ren fooling around with the woman and scolded him in mock anger and surprise. Then he offered the woman to Yi Ren on two conditions, to which Yi Ren readily consented: first, Yi Ren had to marry her, and second, if she bore a son, the son had to be named Yi Ren's legal heir. Eight months later the woman gave birth to a boy.

When the boy was three, Qin troops broke their treaty and attacked the capital of Zhao. The king of Zhao wanted to kill Yi Ren, but Lu Buwei bribed prison guards to let the hostage prince, his wife, and the child escape to Qin. Royal concubine Huayang welcomed them. When the old Qin king died, Yi Ren's father became king but died mysteriously after just three days, whereupon Yi Ren ascended to the throne. Yi Ren made Lu Buwei prime minister and granted him a duke's fiefdom of 100,000 households.

Yi Ren died after only four years on the throne. People suspected Lu Buwei of poisoning both him and his father, but nobody dared make the accusation. The young boy was too little to handle state affairs, so Lu Buwei managed everything. Meanwhile he took up again with the boy's mother, the former singsong girl.

Thus the ambitious merchant took over a state by maneuvering his own people into positions of power. This is the ultimate tale of supplanting beams and pillars with one's own.

However, the rest of the tale shows that this stratagem works only as long as the replacement beams and pillars remain one's own. Lu Buwei's fate illustrates the Chinese adage "Things turn into their opposite when taken to an extreme."

Some years passed and Lu Buwei decided to give up the queen mother, fearing the disapproval of her son, who was coming into his own as a strong and sensible ruler. Lu Buwei concocted an elaborate ruse to smuggle into the palace a loafer renowned for his oversized sex organ. Subsequently the queen mother and her new companion were moved to another city. They had two children, and the loafer was granted a duke's fiefdom. Gradually his influence came to surpass Lu Buwei's. He and the queen mother began plotting to get their son in line for the throne.

News of the plot reached the young ruler, who ordered the loafer arrested and rent asunder by being tied to five oxcarts. The king also dismissed Lu Buwei as prime minister. Ultimately the king recognized Lu Buwei for the knave that he was, and Lu Buwei killed himself rather than face punishment.

The king went on to great things: he conquered the other six kingdoms, reunified China, and in 221 B.C. proclaimed himself emperor of the Qin dynasty—the ruler later known in history as the famous Qin Shihuangdi.

Religious history provides many examples of replacing beams and pillars. Scholars of mythology have noted that many stories, practices, and holy days of Christianity parallel traditional beliefs, customs, and festivals, so that this new system did not seem totally alien to converts from pagan worship. A similar thing occurred with the introduction of Islam. Its founding father Muhammad fled Mecca for the more receptive city of Medina, which adopted his doctrine. Fighting between Mecca and Medina ended in a treaty under which Mecca was to adopt the worship of the Islamic God and accept Muhammad as prophet— but adherents of the new faith would still make pilgrimages to Mecca just as they had done as pagans.

The stratagem of replacing beams and pillars is widely used today in international diplomacy and war. It is a favorite tool of the superpowers. In the years before the invasion of Afghanistan, the Soviet Union sent over 6,000 advisers who gradually took control of the government apparatus. Both superpowers use military and technical aid to gain influence in Third World countries. The U.S. government runs programs for foreign visitors and scholars to cultivate friends abroad.

In a broader sense this stratagem refers to the use of various replacement tactics to achieve one's purposes. In the 1960s when the Japanese determined that high domestic wages made it impossible to compete internationally in the textile industry, they moved their textile manufacturing to lower-wage areas in the Pacific basin and replaced it with electronics. The shift made Japanese textiles more competitive and launched the country on the path to electronics success.

Japanese auto manufacturers responded to pressure from the U.S. government to adopt voluntary quotas with a subtle substitution measure: they upgraded exported cars so that although the volume of exports did not increase, the value did. When the first luxury models from Japan's two biggest automakers began arriving in the United States in 1989, each Toyota Lexus or Nissan Infiniti sold added three times as much to the U.S. trade deficit as the far less expensive vehicle it had replaced. At retail prices of $35,000 to $40,000 per car, it was estimated that these two models could easily add $5 billion to the trade gap by 1992.

When the United States imposed antidumping duties on Japanese computer chips, some Japanese firms exported chips mounted on fake boards since the duties did not apply to mounted chips. This was a less risky approach than smuggling chips in suitcases, which was what some Americans tried.

Accountants frequently use replacement tactics to camouflage problems on the balance sheet. Because the U.S. Federal Reserve Board wants to see six cents of capital for every dollar in loans, savings and loans masquerade mortgages as securities; banks do the same with credit-card receivables; and auto companies do it with car loans. To obscure debt, a company may disguise liabilities as "mandatory redeemable preferred stock."

Transfer pricing is a substitution technique widely used by multinationals. By manipulating prices of transactions between the parent company and subsidiaries or among subsidiaries, a corporation can reallocate taxable income away from high-tax jurisdictions and into low-tax ones, thus reducing its overall tax burden.

Some brokerage houses have profited by using a pillars and beams stratagem that is clearly unethical, if not outright illegal. The stage is set when a broker holds shares in a corporation for a customer, a raider makes a tender for a portion of the stock, and the customer does not reply to the broker's notice inquiring whether the customer wants to tender. Without deleting it from the customer's statement, the broker then transfers some of the customer's shares to a house account and tenders them as the firm's own. When the stock price slumps following the sale, the broker replaces the shares in the customer's account at the reduced price. Having treated the customer's assets as its own, the brokerage house pockets the difference between the tender price and the subsequent trading price, and the customer never knows what he has missed.

The story of how accountants infiltrated the consulting business is another illustration of replacing pillars and beams. It goes back to the advent of computerization in the 1950s when companies turned to auditors for advice on numbers-related problems such as inventory control and payroll management. Gradually the big consulting firms ceded the more tedious tasks and studies to the accounting firms, and later consulting units were set up within the accounting firms. With mergers whittling the once so-called Big Eight of the accounting world into ever-fewer and bigger entities, the consulting arms of these firms may emerge as stronger competitors than ever to the traditional consulting companies.

U.S. unions now regret a substitution commonly agreed to in the concession bargaining of the 1980s when many companies were able to replace raises with bonuses, which are less costly. Raises are folded into base pay and thus count toward pensions, vacation and sick pay, and overtime rates. Most important, raises are compounded by subsequent raises. Bonuses do none of these things. No wonder labor is trying to resubstitute raises for bonuses.

If positions and career patterns at your place of work are not strictly defined, you may be able to parlay your job into something bigger and more remunerative by taking over responsibilities not explicitly claimed by others and gradually enlarging your scope of activity until you become indispensable in those areas. However, you don't want to be taken for granted; you have to make sure that your superiors recognize your contributions and are willing to reward them.

Similarly, to command more respect in your household you may have to move into areas of responsibility that you formerly ignored or left to others. For children, this is part of what growing up is all about. Remarkably, they may find that when they start doing chores without being asked, their parents begin to treat them like human beings.

Kill the chicken to scare the monkey.

—*CHINESE SAYING*

STRATAGEM

26 指桑骂槐

Zhi sang ma huai

Point at the mulberry and curse the locust

THIS STRATAGEM advocates the use of admonitions, scare tactics, clubs, or whatever means necessary to warn, frighten, or beat others into compliance. Essentially, it is a strategy of negative reinforcement. By pointing at the mulberry and cursing the locust, the weak can be cowed and the strong convinced.

Sun Zi, author of the *Art of War*, illustrated the power of this stratagem to the king of Wu, He Lu. When He Lu asked Sun Zi to demonstrate his theories, Sun Zi asserted that he could even train women and children into an invincible army. He Lu then summoned 180 court maidens, whom Sun Zi divided into two columns with the king's two favorite concubines as captains. Then he gave them halberds and explained the maneuvers they were expected to perform in accord with particular drumbeats. But when he beat the drum ordering a right turn, they merely giggled. Even after he explained several more times, when he beat the drum for a left turn they giggled again.

Sun Zi said it must be the captains' fault and ordered the two concubines beheaded. He appointed the women at the front of the two columns to be the new captains. This time when he beat the drum, the maidens performed exactly as directed.

At He Lu's heartsick reaction to his achievement, Sun Zi only said, "Your Majesty loves the words in my book but can't stomach putting them into practice." Eventually, however, He Lu appointed Sun Zi as his chief commander.

The United States' dropping of atomic bombs on Hiroshima and Nagasaki was a modern application of this stratagem—and one that took the stratagem to extremes. Some believe that dropping a single bomb, and on a noncivilian target, might have sent the message with far less human suffering. Indeed, some historians argue that the use of atomic weapons was not necessary at all.

Companies with turf to protect often point at the mulberry and abuse the locust to ward off potential incursions. For instance, when Polaroid and Kodak make moves into each other's areas of expertise—namely, instant and conventional photography respectively—in part each is warning the other to stay in its own market. Computer hardware and software companies have a penchant for filing lawsuits charging patent and copyright infringements. At an early stage this tactic can be an effective warning against copycats, though if violations proliferate it becomes meaningless.

Most legal systems work in part on the assumption that negative examples will deter crime. When merger mania reached a peak in the United States in the mid-1980s, a great deal more insider trading than actually came to light was undoubtedly taking place. By publicizing and prosecuting several prominent cases—Levine, Boesky, Milken—the SEC sent a strong message to others who might be tempted into such white-collar crimes.

Modern business managers prefer to use positive reinforcement to encourage their personnel—commendations, money, and other psychological and material rewards. However, negative examples may have to be made of some people under some circumstances not only to handle those individual cases but to keep those situations from arising again. The same holds true in child rearing: children in elementary school don't need personal experience to learn that unruly behavior leads to deprivation of recess or a trip to the principal's office.

A man of great wisdom often
appears slow-witted.
—CHINESE SAYING

STRATAGEM

27 俊癡不癲

Jia chi bu dian

Play dumb while remaining smart

THE SMARTEST PEOPLE do not always let on how smart they
are. The less smart who think they are smart often act
recklessly when it would be wiser to feign foolishness while
biding their time. This is the rationale behind playing
dumb while remaining smart. The idea is reflected in the
Book of Changes hexagram number 3, meaning to advance
slowly, which implies that any forward movement should
be undertaken only after careful consideration.

Playing dumb while remaining smart plays on the yin-
yang interaction between movement and stillness, secrecy
and openness, action and reaction. In line with Sun Zi's
teaching that "When one is strong, one should pretend to
be weak," it is a method for making the enemy underestimate you.

155

The stratagem is illustrated by the story of how Liu Bei, a much beloved leader living two millennia ago, extricated himself from the clutches of his ruthless rival Cao Cao. In A.D. 198 Liu Bei was defeated by a warlord and sought asylum with Cao Cao, who was then prime minister of the Han court. Cao Cao granted Liu Bei the title of duke and treated him generously but in fact kept him under a kind of house arrest. Cao Cao's true purpose was to control the increasingly popular and influential Liu Bei.

Meanwhile Cao Cao was also scheming to usurp power from the young Han emperor Xiandi. When Xiandi realized this, he wrote a secret edict in his own blood vowing to work toward Cao Cao's death. Liu Bei secretly joined in the plot but avoided attracting suspicion by staying at his residence and cultivating a vegetable garden.

One day Cao Cao came to visit Liu Bei. They sat at a stone table in a small pavilion surrounded by plum trees and talked over wine and food. The sky was overcast, and it looked as though it was going to rain. Cao Cao asked Liu Bei, "You have been to many places and met many people. Can you tell me who the heroes of today are?" Liu Bei listed numerous lords and leaders, but Cao Cao scoffed at each name and finally said that only Liu Bei and himself could be called true heroes.

Liu Bei, sure that Cao Cao had seen through him, felt so startled that he dropped his chopsticks on the ground. Just at that moment, a thunder clap resounded. Liu Bei quickly explained that the thunder had scared him and made his hands shake. From this incident, Cao Cao assumed that Liu Bei was a coward. Soon after, his guard let down, Cao Cao let Liu Bei march away at the head of 50,000 soldiers to fight a warlord. Needless to say, Liu Bei did not plan to come back. He told a close associate, "I have been living like a bird in the cage and a fish in the net. Now I am like a fish swimming back to sea and a bird soaring into the sky." Subsequently Cao Cao discovered the plot against him and executed most of those who had signed the edict, but by then Liu Bei was far away.

Interestingly, the stratagem of playing dumb has been used by military leaders to fool their own troops on numerous occasions in Chinese history. This finds endorsement in Sun Zi's suggestion that commanders may need to hoodwink soldiers to keep military plans confidential. Another reason was to keep troops in good spirits. Liu Bang, founder of the Western Han dynasty, was once shot in the chest in battle. Knowing that news of such a serious wound would damage his men's morale, he cried out that he had been shot in the toe. A thousand years later during the Song dynasty, General Di Qing prepared his men for a particularly difficult battle by tossing a hundred coins and telling them that a hundred heads would signify imminent victory. Although his advisers protested, saying the results could not possibly come out thus, he tossed the coins anyway and they all came out heads up. His soldiers won the battle and returned to discover that the coins had been specially minted with heads on both sides.

In business affairs, playing dumb is a way to disarm others who might be inclined to attack. The stratagem is particularly useful in business negotiations when you don't want to let on how much you really know about the other side's plans. But bear in mind that the other side may be playing dumb too!

For companies associated with the latest in modern technology and management, appearing dumb while remaining smart may take the form of using old-fashioned promotional methods. It is not surprising that U.S. Sprint spent tens of millions of dollars on ads portraying itself as a technologically advanced alternative to AT&T. But the company also enlisted a force of 30,000 part-time salespeople to peddle its long-distance phone service at street corners, county fairs, and shopping malls.

Appearing dumb when you actually are smart is not always so easy. Women have an advantage in this regard because of the common male assumption that women are less capable or intelligent than men. Sandra Kurtzig, who at age twenty-four founded Ask Computer Systems, a Silicon Valley software company, and at forty-two stepped down as chairwoman of the $200 million enterprise to write her autobiography, is a case in point. Being a woman helped her succeed, she says, because men didn't regard her as real competition and readily gave her advice and directed business her way.

Playing dumb can serve several functions in personal relationships. When you are just getting to know someone, playing dumb will induce the person to reveal more about his or her character. If you want to inject levity into a relationship, acting ignorant and then revealing the joke is a harmless way to tease. If your spouse or child always waits to hear how you think before expressing an opinion or making a decision, playing dumb can help encourage them to think for themselves.

*Faced with death, he who is ready
to die will survive while he who is
determined to live will die.*
—*Qing dynasty strategist Wu Zheng*

STRATAGEM

28 上屋抽梯

Shang wu chou ti

*Pull down the ladder after
the ascent*

THIS STRATAGEM can be interpreted in several ways, but the most common meaning is to lure the enemy into a trap and then cut off his escape route. Different types of adversaries may be lured in different ways—the greedy enemy with the promise of gain, the arrogant enemy with a sign of weakness, the inflexible enemy by a ruse.

Pulling down the ladder also may mean plunging one's own supporters or potential allies into a crisis situation that forces them to come up with novel solutions to problems. The Spanish explorer Cortez used this stratagem when he burned his own ships upon arriving in what is today Veracruz, Mexico, to prevent his men from pressuring him to return home. They had the choice of conquering or perishing—and conquer they did.

Liu Qi, beleaguered heir to a fiefdom during the Three Kingdoms period, once pulled down a ladder to force the famed Zhuge Liang, brilliant adviser to the leader Liu Bei, to help him out.

The eldest son of a warlord who had given Liu Bei asylum, Liu Qi came to Liu Bei for help in warding off a challenge from his stepmother and his half brother. Liu Bei wanted to assist, but when he asked Zhuge Liang for advice, Zhuge Liang refused to intervene in what he saw as a family matter.

Nonetheless, Liu Bei dispatched Zhuge Liang to visit Liu Qi the next day. Following Liu Bei's instructions, Liu Qi lured Zhuge Liang to the second story of a building by promising him a look at a rare ancient book. When Zhuge Liang returned to the staircase to leave, he found the stairs had been removed. This time he complied with Liu Qi's pleas for help, providing him with a plan for escaping death at the hands of his relatives.

Pulling down the ladder to force one's own supporters into decisive action can be seen in a story about the consolidation of the Western Han dynasty. After setting up the dynasty, Liu Bang sent his best general, Han Xin, to quell the still defiant fiefdom of Zhao in North China. First, Han Xin quietly sent two cavalry divisions to flank the Zhao campsite. Meanwhile he ordered 10,000 troops to cross a river and form a battle formation with their backs to the river, violating a well-known principle of troop deployment.

Next, Han Xin sent one division out in a brief show of fighting. Then he had his soldiers beat a disorderly retreat, luring the enemy into pursuit. Having set up the formation on the river so his troops could pull back no farther, Han Xin shouted that they had no way out but to fight. When pressed into this trap laid by their own commander, Han Xin's troops indeed fought desperately.

The astonished Zhao troops fell back to their camp only to find thousands of Han banners there fluttering in the breeze. The banners had been planted by the cavalry troops hiding nearby, but the Zhao soldiers thought the camp had been overrun, and they fled in all directions. The Zhao commander was killed in the melee, and the recalcitrant Zhao king captured.

The technique Han Xin employed on his troops has parallels in the business world. "Management by crisis," or the practice of plunging an enterprise into a precarious situation to provoke a desired response, is based on the premise that under critical conditions people are quicker to make decisions, more creative in solving problems, more resolute in assuming hard tasks, and more willing to tolerate hardships than in normal times. Management by crisis is a sometimes risky but often effective means for stimulating employees' enthusiasm, responsibility, and productivity.

Frank Lorenzo used this approach in the fall of 1983 when his financially troubled Continental Airlines filed for bankruptcy. The drastic move enabled him to break labor contracts, slash his work force, cut salaries, and unilaterally implement new wage and work rules. Today, Continental has regained health and is a viable contender in air passenger transport. By the time he tried to do the same with Eastern Airlines, however, employees knew the game plan and resisted him.

The high labor efficiency in modern capitalist countries can be attributed in part to a more general crisis effect—the threat of unemployment. Job insecurity makes people work harder. The leadership of mainland China recently rediscovered this fact and as part of its market-oriented reforms is gradually phasing out the practice of lifetime job tenure.

Removing the ladder, when turned upon oneself, can be a means to impress, or shock, or make a point. The daredevils who cross Niagara Falls on a tightrope or rappel down the World Trade Center represent extreme cases of this; they leave themselves no escape from their death-defying displays.

The effectiveness of this stratagem rests on its inexorableness. In pulling away the ladder, you engineer a situation in which the consequences, though created by you, are no longer under your control. Crisis in the workplace is just as likely to undermine morale as it is to stimulate innovation. Declaring bankruptcy may damage your company's image irreversibly even if it bails you out. Unemployment in an economic system may lead to political unrest. And of course one can fall off a tightrope. Therefore, one should use this stratagem with one's eyes wide open, aware that it could backfire.

> *A crafty fox caught by a hungry tiger protested, "You dare not eat me because I am superior to all other animals, and if you eat me you will anger the gods. If you don't believe me, just follow me and see what happens." The tiger followed the fox into the woods, and all the animals ran away at the first sight of them. The awed tiger, not realizing he was the cause of alarm, let the fox go.* —CHINESE FABLE

STRATAGEM

29 樹上开花

Shu shang kai hua

Deck the tree with bogus blossoms

THIS STRATAGEM provides a way to present a powerful face even if your actual forces are minimal. The expression that describes it originated with Emperor Yangdi of the Sui dynasty (A.D. 581–618), famed for building the Grand Canal but also notorious for his debauchery and ostentatious lifestyle.

Yangdi often organized huge concerts with as many as 18,000 musicians performing at once. To impress traveling merchants from Central Asia, he ordered restaurateurs not to charge the visitors and to tell them that China was so rich that diners never had to pay for their food. In the winter the emperor ordered all the bare trees in the capital of Loyang decked with silk flowers to mimic spring.

All these ruses failed to fool the visitors, who asked why

163

the emperor didn't use the silk to clothe the ragged beggars in the streets. Thenceforth, decking the tree with bogus blossoms came to mean pretending to be more than one really is.

A maestro of putting up false flowers to put down rebellion was Yu Xu, an official during the Eastern Han dynasty. When he was assigned to govern the city of Wudu, the Qiang minority tribe tried to block his arrival at a pass. So he leaked word that he had called on the court for reinforcements, and the rebels went off to nearby towns to do some looting while waiting for the reinforcements. Yu Xu easily broke through the now weakly defended pass.

When the rebels heard, they returned to give chase. Yu Xu managed to confuse the pursuers terribly by ordering his soldiers to double the number of campfires they built each time they stopped for meals, and they safely reached Wudu. About 3,000 Qiang troops were waiting at Wudu, but some 10,000 had besieged the nearby city of Chiting, so Yu Xu sent out a detachment to lure those at Chiting to Wudu. As the Qiang rebels approached Wudu, Yu Xu's men ineffectively shot puny arrows from small bows which emboldened the Qiang to come closer. Just as the Qiang were about to storm the city, Yu Xu's soldiers released a barrage of arrows from enormous crossbows, felling all the rebels in the front ranks and scaring the rest off.

The next day Yu Xu ordered all four gates of Wudu swung open. He sent all his troops out of the city through the north gate and had them come in again through the east gate, whereupon they changed their uniforms and then went out the north gate and in the east gate again. At the sight of what they thought were far more troops than they had originally imagined, the Qiang rebels began to withdraw. They fell right into an ambush and were routed. Never again did the Qiang tangle with Yu Xu.

The adding of stoves and the promenading in and out of the city were applications of decking the tree with bogus blossoms, designed to make forces look stronger than they really were. The use of minimal firepower also employed this stratagem but to give an impression of weakness. Generally the stratagem is used by the weak to fend off the strong. Of course the strong can present itself as even stronger to deter competitors or as weaker to lead adversaries astray.

Mao Zedong may well have been thinking of putting false flowers on the tree in his overtures to the United States in the early 1970s. In light of Sino-Soviet border tensions, Mao welcomed this new relationship that perhaps would cloak China with more power than it really had.

Throughout the Cold War period, Americans and Soviets were so distrustful of each other that each side assumed the other was always decking the trees with false blossoms. Even though the antagonistic rhetoric has abated, in some quarters the distrust persists. Some American analysts still argue that the Soviet Union's pullout from Afghanistan, new laissez-faire stance toward Eastern Europe, and ambitious attempts at *glasnost* and *perestroika* are all part of a master plan to lull the West into a false sense of security. Increasingly, however, U.S. opinion leaders—from Secretary of State James Baker to Pepsico chairman Donald Kendall—see these as real blossoms, not false ones.

Politics and diplomacy still provide plenty of opportunity for fanciful claims that may not accord with reality. A U.S. State Department official in the Bush administration, Francis Fukuyama, became an instant darling of neoconservatives with the publication of his article entitled "The End of History," but critics said his arguments were absurd. Veteran *Time* magazine correspondent Strobe Talbott renamed the article "The Beginning of Nonsense."

In business, decking the trees with bogus blossoms can be used as a marketing tool. A company that tries to generate the appearance of demand for a fledgling new product when customer awareness of the product may not yet exist is using this stratagem. The Japanese electronics company Sanyo, when it introduced a radio with an injected plastic shell in 1952 to lukewarm dealer response, dispatched salespersons disguised as customers specifically looking for that model radio. Within two years, sales doubled and Sanyo's market share for radios grew to No. 2, after National.

Decking the tree with bogus blossoms is of course a tried and tested trick for résumé writers. Rather than writing that you spent a summer crewing on your Uncle Joe's boat, you put that you "successfully implemented regional navigational strategy." However, you should avoid excessive embroidering: a prospective employer generally notices when something rings too good to be true.

Stretching the truth in order present oneself in the best light may be a universal human tendency and one encouraged by American individualism and competitiveness. But understatement can make just as strong an impression. In fact, people who are evaluating you as a person or prospective employee may find modesty a refreshing change. In job applications, keep your letters short and straightforward and let your references, transcripts, and track record speak for themselves. In forming friendships, let your personality and actions represent you. Sometimes stripping the tree to the bare branches may be more effective than prettifying it. And afterward, nobody can accuse you of misleading them.

The best defense is an offense.
—CHINESE SAYING

STRATAGEM

30 反客為主

Fan ke wei zhu

Make the host and the guest exchange places

IN CHINESE MILITARY TERMINOLOGY, one who ventures out of his own territory to fight is the "guest" and one who defends his own territory, the "host." The relations between guest and host may be of varying types. Sometimes the guest is in a strong position, invited to help out a weak host. Sometimes the guest is weak and must rely temporarily on a strong host. Usually the host has the advantageous position because he is familiar with the terrain and the local situation.

The host typically concentrates on crippling the guest's logistics, while the guest takes aim at the host's headquarters. The guest can change places with the host in a variety of ways—by building up his forces until he is strong enough to overcome the host, by infiltrating the host in the guise of friendship, then gradually taking over control, or by moving into the territory after luring the host out.

A popular Beijing opera, *Xiang Yu Bids Farewell to Yuji*, tells a story that resulted from Liu Bang's application of this stratagem. Xiang Yu and Liu Bang both were leaders of rebellions against the Qin Dynasty. By clever maneuvering, Liu Bang deflected the major forces of the Qin army and entered the Qin capital while Xiang Yu was entrenched in a major battle elsewhere. The Qin emperor surrendered to Liu Bang with a noose of white ribbon around his neck and the jade seal of state in his hand.

Once a lowly village chieftain, Liu Bang was dazzled by the magnificence of the imperial palace and enchanted by the beauty of the court maidens. But as he was about to settle down for a night of enjoyment, an adviser admonished him not to do anything that might damage his reputation. The adviser said that Xiang Yu held the advantage with four times as many troops and Liu Bang could not afford to alienate public opinion. In fact, Xiang Yu was the "host" and Liu Bang was only a "guest."

Liu Bang agreed with this reasoning. He left the palace, withdrew his troops to a nearby city, and issued edicts that strengthened the rule of law while doing away with the harsh laws of the Qin. He pretended that he had no intention of trying to take over the throne. Soon afterwards, he let Xiang Yu take the capital without opposition.

Within a few years, Liu Bang had built up his army and felt strong enough. The decisive battle was waged in what is now Anhui province in central China. Overpowered, Xiang Yu prepared to flee. His favorite concubine, Yuji, slit her throat with his sword so as not to burden him, and as he was fleeing he also decided life was no longer worth living and killed himself with the same sword.

In modern times we have seen several large-scale examples of the guest supplanting the host. The Americans in Vietnam, the Vietnamese in Cambodia, and the Soviets in Afghanistan all claimed to have been invited guests and all assumed a hostlike, directive role in those countries' affairs. When the government of Sri Lanka invited in the

Having been bested by Liu Bang's use of the stratagem "making the host and the guest exchange places," Xiang Yu bids adieu to his favorite concubine Yuji, who has slit her throat, and prepares to do the same.

Indian army as a peacekeeping force to help quell Tamil rebels in the north, the numbers of Indian soldiers and police in that small island nation soon swelled to rival native forces. Under such a situation, it would not be hard for the guest to exchange places with the host.

The business world is an arena where hosts and guests exchange places constantly. When executives falter, their underlings generally move in to succeed them. A well-known example of this is the case of John Sculley, chairman and CEO of Apple Computer. Sculley originally came to that firm as a guest. The host was founder Steve Jobs. Sculley became increasingly critical of Jobs's management, and Jobs became increasingly vulnerable as the company's financial health took a downturn. Finally, Sculley edged Jobs out to become the host.

Companies filling specialized niches in the computer industry often begin as guests and turn into hosts. Manufacturers of linking devices such as workstations and servers introduce products compatible with existing machines so that customers can easily fit them into their existing systems. If the devices catch on, eventually new systems will be built around them with other machines as the add-ons.

Making the host and guest exchange places can come in useful in everyday human relations. Throughout life you are a guest in the territory of a great many hosts—your parents, your teachers, your boss, sometimes even your spouse. At times only small gestures are needed to balance the situation. If you bring your professor a cup of coffee, it helps equalize the relationship. If you invite your supervisor over to dinner, it may be easier to ask him for that raise. If you take your wife or husband to the movies, you have seized the initiative.

In domestic affairs, women tend to fall easily into the host role, sometimes without even noticing. Both partners may be comfortable with this setup until a change occurs in their lives—the woman gets a more demanding job, a newborn arrives, the children leave home, the man retires. The ideal situation, of course, is for everyone to take turns being guest and host.

SIX

STRATAGEMS
FOR
DESPERATE
STRAITS

*These stratagems are designed with the
weak in mind. They may be last resorts
in an emergency. They call for hitting
below the belt, for bluster and bravado,
and even for self-destructiveness. If the
first five of these fail, one can always
try the last—running away. Good luck!*

> No man can break through the
> Pass of Beauties.
> —*CHINESE SAYING*

STRATAGEM

31 美人計

Mei ren ji

Use a woman to ensnare a man

THIS STRATAGEM has been used from time immemorial. When you face a strong, resolute, and resourceful enemy, the lure of the opposite sex may be the only way to break his will. In a more general sense, using a woman to ensnare a man means presenting your adversary with any sort of irresistible temptation. Britain conquered China's coastline with gunboats in the mid-eighteenth century, but it was opium that kept the Chinese enslaved over the next hundred years.

China's history is full of lascivious men whose weakness for women led to their downfall. Dong Zhuo, the ruthless military strongman who usurped the power of the Eastern Han court (see Stratagem 14), met such a fate—and deservedly so.

173

Dong Zhuo was supremely cruel as well as debauched. In A.D. 190, he conscripted 250,000 laborers to build him a magnificent city and enlisted 800 young beauties to serve in his palace there. The next year he forced the puppet child-emperor Xiandi to appoint him top imperial adviser. With great spectacle and fanfare, he would travel back and forth between his city and the imperial capital of Chang-an—present-day Xian. He often held huge parties in tents outside the capital, where he demanded increasingly grisly and sadistic entertainment. Once he had several hundred captives tortured to death before his guests—their eyes gouged out, ears torn off, and noses and penises amputated. Later he began wanton killing of court officials. The executioner was the mightiest warrior of the time, Lu Bu, whom Dong Zhuo had won over with gold and horses and adopted like a son.

A high official in the Han court named Wang Yun began to think about how to defeat Dong Zhuo. Dong Zhuo seemed invincible—he always wore his armor inside his robes, and the intimidating Lu Bu was often at his side. The strongman already had repulsed several challengers.

Wang Yun was at his wits' end until one sleepless night when he was strolling in his garden and came upon the comely, sixteen-year-old singsong girl named Diaochan, whom he had raised like a daughter since childhood, praying before an incense burner. Diaochan had noticed her master's distraction and wanted to help him. He poured out his worries to her, and together they laid a plot to rid the land of the tyrant.

As a first step, Wang Yun sent Lu Bu a gold crown inlaid with pearls. The delighted Lu Bu came in person to thank Wang Yun, who threw a feast for him and flattered him profusely. After a few goblets of wine, Wang Yun called in Diaochan and she enthralled Lu Bu. Wang Yun said she was his youngest daughter and offered her hand to Lu Bu. Lu Bu immediately accepted. Wang Yun said he would choose a lucky date to send her over.

A few days later when Lu Bu was not around, Wang Yun

invited Dong Zhuo for a meal. The strongman arrived with a battalion of bodyguards. Dong Zhuo and Wang Yun ate and drank from noon until evening, and then Wang Yun took Dong Zhuo into a back room and summoned Diaochan to sing and dance. Dong Zhuo was no less enchanted than Lu Bu had been. Wang Yun offered her to him also, and Dong Zhuo took her home that very day.

Learning that Diaochan was with Dong Zhuo, Lu Bu angrily confronted Wang Yun. Wang Yun explained that Dong Zhuo knew about the betrothal and was merely picking the bride up for Lu Bu because it was an auspicious day. He assured Lu Bu that the bride and her dowry would be in hand in a few more days. Meanwhile Dong Zhuo consorted with Diaochan and fell deeper and deeper in love.

Diaochan proved masterful at playing Lu Bu and Dong Zhuo off against each other. When Lu Bu finally got the chance to see her alone, she pretended that Dong Zhuo had forced her to serve him. Lu Bu vowed to save her. When Dong Zhuo discovered them embracing and Lu Bu ran off, she pretended that Lu Bu had tried to violate her by force. Dong Zhuo vowed to protect her.

Wang Yun subtly encouraged the disconsolate Lu Bu to assert his claim over Diaochan. So one spring day when Dong Zhuo arrived in the capital for a meeting with the young emperor, Lu Bu slit Dong Zhuo's throat. The evil strongman's head was presented to the emperor, and the body incinerated in the street.

Thus Diaochan saved the kingdom from further oppression by this tyrant. However, she was unable to save the Han dynasty. Her master was killed by troops loyal to Dong Zhuo, and she disappeared amid the warfare of the times. Another strongman, Cao Cao, finally caught and executed Lu Bu and seized control of the throne. The Eastern Han dynasty would soon die out, to be replaced by the era of the Three Kingdoms.

Diaochan's mission was a murderous one, but other women in Chinese history have served pacific goals. One Han emperor sent his court beauty Zhaojun as a peace offering to the chieftain of the powerful nomadic Huns. And Emperor Taizong of the Tang dynasty forged a famous alliance in A.D. 680 by sending his daughter Princess Wencheng to marry the king of ancient Tibet.

Alexander the Great tried a similar tactic to keep peace in the ranks of his own army: after conquering Central Asia in the fourth century B.C., he first attempted to win over his new subjects by assuming the robe and crown of a Persian monarch. However, this aroused jealousy among his Macedonian commanders. So he arranged a number of marriages between these officers and Persian and Babylonian women. Unfortunately he never lived to see the unity he sought—after a drinking bout in Babylon, he ran a fever and died in 323 B.C., whereupon his vast dominion fell apart.

In modern espionage, using a woman to ensnare a man—or a man to ensnare a woman—has proven a powerful tool. In one of the most celebrated spy cases of recent years, the American Richard Miller, a former FBI agent, was charged with selling secrets to his Soviet lover, who along with her husband pleaded guilty to espionage. In another case, the Israeli secret service reportedly used a Druze woman to lure a Syrian air force pilot who defected with a Soviet-built fighter plane.

This stratagem has been used as a tool of assassination as well. When the Sandinistas were fighting to overthrow the Nicaraguan dictator Anastasio Somoza, they used a woman to lure one of Somoza's top generals into a death trap.

We now know that presidents as well-respected as Franklin D. Roosevelt and John F. Kennedy had extramarital flings. Even the venerated Martin Luther King, Jr. violated his own proscriptions against sex outside the marriage—and the FBI came close to blackmailing him on this account. In this age of tell-all journalism, revelations about liaisons can be devastating. Gary Hart, discovered in the company of a woman who was not his wife, dropped out of the 1988 Democratic presidential primaries. Massachusetts congressman Barney Frank, bright, liberal, and an acknowledged homosexual, faced the greatest crisis of his career in 1989 after a former partner presented a sordid account of their relationship. While these events were not necessarily Republican plots, they at least provided political adversaries with cause for glee.

The most obvious commercial application of using a woman to ensnare a man is the ubiquitous use of sexy models or allusions to sex in advertising. The more general form of this stratagem, using temptations of all varieties, is evident whenever business dealings are greased by kickbacks or bribes of any sort.

The use of temptation to trap people may be defensible in some circumstances, but it can also boomerang because it is easily seen as unfair. In 1982 millions of Americans watching network television saw John DeLorean participating in a $60-million drug deal that had turned out to be an FBI sting. His acquittal on the charges was probably due in part to the jury's uneasiness at the idea of the government's setting him up. Jurors were also ambivalent in the case of accused spy Richard Miller—his first trial ended in an acquittal, and though he was convicted a second time around he won in a third trial over faulty admission of lie-detector test results as evidence. Similar ambivalence attended the cocaine-sting trial of Washington, D.C., mayor Marion Barry.

Using inducements to win friends and influence people is even more questionable. Holding out rewards to your children may appear as an effective technique for getting them to do things in the short run, but children who grow accustomed to such barter will have a harder time developing self-esteem and moral justification for their behavior in the long run. And other relationships that operate on a quid pro quo basis can never develop into anything very deep and trusting.

> *Make a void appear hollow and
> your enemy will suspect that you
> are really solid.*
>
> *—STRATAGEMS OF*
> *THE THATCHED HOUSE*
> *(CAOLU JINGLUE)*

STRATAGEM

32 空城什

Kong cheng ji

*Fling open the gates to the
empty city*

THIS STRATAGEM is to be used when you are in a thoroughly vulnerable situation. Its success hinges on the propensity of people to suspect what is willingly acknowledged. If you have absolutely no means of defense and you openly reveal this situation to the enemy, he is likely to assume the opposite.

This ruse takes its name from one of the most memorable feats of Zhuge Liang, the great strategist who lived at the time when the Eastern Han dynasty was disintegrating and the Three Kingdoms were rising to take its place. As adviser to Liu Bei, Zhuge Liang had mapped out the plans that led to the creation of the kingdom of Shu in southwest China. Subsequently he became prime minister of Shu. In this post, he led five expeditions against the kingdom of Wei,

ruled by Liu Bei's archrival Cao Cao. On one of those expeditions, in A.D. 228, he used the strategy of flinging open
the gates to the empty city to deter what otherwise would
have been a devastating assault.

To block Zhuge Liang's advance, the Wei commander
Sima Yi attacked the small but strategic town of Jieting.
The Shu general who volunteered to take charge of the
town's defense had built an encampment atop a hill that
proved a catastrophic mistake: Sima Yi easily surrounded
the camp and cut off the water supply, forcing the parched
Shu soldiers to break through their own ramparts to surrender. Alarmed at the loss of Jieting, Zhuge Liang sent
some of his troops into retreat, keeping only 2,500 men at
his headquarters in the city of Xicheng. Meanwhile Sima
Yi continued on toward Xicheng with a force of 150,000,
determined to capture the Shu strategist.

Zhuge Liang was stupefied when he mounted the city
wall and saw two long trails of dust rising like dragons in
the distance. Immediately he ordered all the Shu banners
lowered and the four gates to the city flung wide open. At
each gate he assigned twenty soldiers disguised as civilians
to sweep the streets. He instructed all the rest of his soldiers
to hide in the sentry posts on top of the city wall; anybody
who showed himself or spoke aloud would be beheaded on
the spot. Then Zhuge Liang himself, dressed in a long flow-
ing robe, mounted the city wall, sat down before the main
watchtower, and began to play the lute. Two pages stood
beside him, one holding a sword, the other a feather duster.

When Sima Yi's vanguard troops arrived and saw Zhuge
Liang lost in his music and apparently unconcerned about
possible attack, they dared not enter the city. Sima Yi did
not believe their report and rushed up on horseback to see
with his own eyes. Sure enough, he found Zhuge Liang
playing melodious music atop the city wall while what he
assumed were city residents were calmly sweeping the
streets below. Concluding that the peaceful scene could
only mean that a terrible trap lay in store for him, he ordered an immediate retreat.

Zhuge Liang led his army safely back to the Shu capital, where he insisted on having himself demoted three ranks for the defeat at Jieting.

Flinging open the gates to the empty city is a risky form of bluffing. You claim to be no more than what you are and hope that others will imagine you to be a great deal more.

Players in a competitive business environment have a natural preference for secrecy and surprise. But occasionally a company can get a leg up on a competitor by using candor. Few manufacturers are willing to make fun of themselves, but the founders of the odd menagerie known as Teenage Mutant Ninja Turtles—toy figurines that have caught on like wildfire among preteen boys—have enhanced their product line's rambunctious image by publicizing how the whole enterprise began as a lark.

Sometimes flinging open the gates to the empty city may be a genuine effort to convince others that what they see is what they get. Politicians generally exaggerate both promises and achievements, so the occasional statesman or stateswoman who actually means what he or she says can make a great impression. For several years the United States did not take Gorbachev's peace overtures at face value; for instance, when the Soviet Union initiated a unilateral test ban, the United States did not accept the invitation to follow suit, and after extending the ban once the Soviets subsequently resumed testing. By late 1989, however, American officials were beginning to think that perhaps the city was empty after all. Secretary of State James Baker, in a speech on arms control, declared that Gorbachev's reforms provided "the clearest opportunity to reduce the risk of war since the dawn of the nuclear age."

This stratagem suggests that in your workday life openness about weaknesses may be read as a sign of confidence and strength. The boss will respect someone who admits to problems more than someone who tries to cover them up, colleagues will appreciate that someone else is willing to acknowledge the problems, friends will do all they can to help you overcome them, and adversaries will not believe that things are really as bad as you say.

> *How delicate! How subtle! There
> are no situations in which spies
> cannot be used.*
> —Sun Zi, THE ART OF WAR

STRATAGEM

33 反间计

Fan jian ji

*Let the enemy's own spy sow
discord in the enemy camp*

ESPIONAGE MAY BE the second-oldest profession, but the basics have not changed much since Sun Zi devoted a whole chapter to the subject 2,500 years ago. Spying, double agentry, and counterintelligence techniques were employed by contending warlords in ancient China at least as commonly as they are now by the national intelligence-gathering agencies of modern states.

This stratagem advocates manipulating your adversary's own agents to serve your purposes. The quintessential example of letting the enemy's own spy sow discord in the enemy camp is the tale of Jiang Gan, who unwittingly sabotaged the well-laid plans of his master Cao Cao.

Like so many of these classic military stories, this one dates from the contentious times when the Eastern Han dynasty was dying and the Three Kingdoms were in formation. Cao Cao, who had gained control over the Han throne and would found the kingdom of Wei, was preparing to cross the Yangtze River to fight his rivals to the south—Liu Bei, founder of the kingdom of Shu, and Sun Quan, head of the kingdom of Wu. These two had formed a temporary alliance to resist Cao Cao.

Sun Quan's troops would face the first onslaught when Cao Cao's forces crossed the river. Though Cao Cao's troops outnumbered Sun Quan's by more than ten to one, Sun Quan's men had the advantage of knowing how to fight on water. Cao Cao's soldiers, being northerners, had no experience in battling from boats. After a skirmish on the river, Cao Cao decided that his troops needed naval training. He put two generals who had defected from Wu in charge of the job.

Cao Cao also sent an emissary to investigate the other side's preparations. This was Jiang Gan, who happened to be a former schoolmate of Sun Quan's commander Zhou Yu. Jiang Gan crossed the river on the pretext of visiting an old friend. Zhou Yu pretended to believe him and entertained him in grand style, plying him with liquor and all the while emphasizing their comradeship. This talk plus the sight of Zhou Yu's confident officers and troops made Jiang Gan increasingly nervous.

When Jiang Gan finally asked to retire, Zhou Yu insisted they share a bed. Zhou Yu flung himself down fully dressed and fell into a drunken stupor, but Jiang Gan could not sleep. Instead he got up to rifle through the papers on Zhou Yu's desk. Among them was a letter bearing the signatures of the two generals Cao Cao had hired as naval trainers revealing a plot to kill Cao Cao. The alarmed Jiang Gan took the letter and returned to the bed, only to hear Zhou Yu mumble in his sleep, "Jiang Gan, in a few days I'll show you Cao Cao's head."

At dawn Jiang Gan slipped away and returned across the river, where he showed Cao Cao the letter. The enraged Cao Cao summoned the two generals and ordered them be-

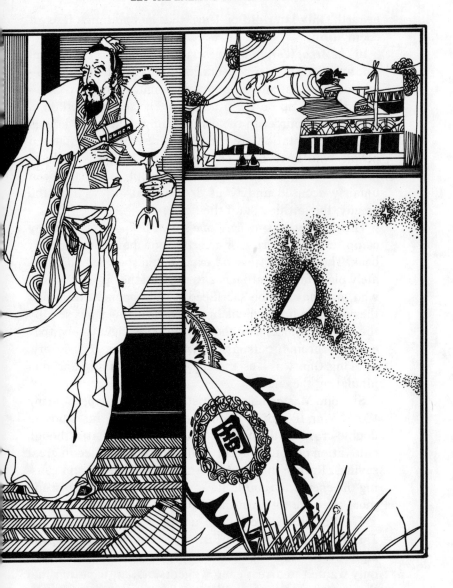

Zhou Yu makes use of Cao Cao's spy Jiang Gan to "sow discord in the enemy camp"; Jiang Gan arises from bed and finds a letter planted by Zhou Yu that incriminates two of Cao Cao's generals, and Cao Cao subsequently executes the generals on the basis of this trumped-up information.

headed. Only later did he learn that he had fallen into an enemy trap.

In *The Art of War*, Sun Zi described five types of espionage. One approach is to enlist connections in the enemy camp— friends, fellows, and former schoolmates who have happened to end up on the other side. The second method is to buy over sources in the enemy camp. Likely candidates for such co-optation are those with resentments: talented people who have been shunted aside, people who have made mistakes and been punished, people who have been unfairly accused and want exoneration—as well as the greedy, the faithless, and the fickle.

The third way is to send one's own people to the enemy camp, either covertly or overtly, and have them report back. The fourth is to send expendable spies who deliberately plant false intelligence to mislead the opposition and who may have to be sacrificed if the opponent discovers the ruse. The final type is buying or utilizing spies sent by the enemy. Sun Zi saw the use of double agents—be they enlisted through persuasion, with money, or by trickery, as Jiang Gan was—as the key to understanding and manipulating the enemy.

Sir John Masterman, a British intelligence expert during World War II, would undoubtedly agree. In his study of double-crossing during the war, he noted that although cultivation of double agents took effort, it resulted in great savings. Rather than suppressing enemy agents and causing the enemy to rebuild its spy network, it is cheaper and more effective to "turn them around."

The British double agent Dusko Popov complained that J. Edgar Hoover and the FBI never understood this principle. In his book *Spy/Counterspy*, he said the Americans only wanted to arrest enemy agents, not anticipating that the enemy would immediately replace them with new agents.

Industrial espionage relies heavily on inside agents. Most such endeavors never come to light, but in the high-stakes world of high tech, opportunities for both sellers and buyers abound. IBM enlisted the FBI in a sting operation that trapped would-be purchasers of industrial secrets in 1982: instead of receiving confidential documents from the source they thought they had bought over, two engineers from the Japanese electronics firm Hitachi found themselves being read their legal rights. As the scandal unfolded, thirteen Hitachi employees were indicted, and their company ended up settling with IBM for $300 million. An ancient Chinese schemer might have taken the plan to more malicious extremes such as supplying the Hitachi agents with false information. However, IBM did not go that far.

A milder form of business double agentry is when people in the know defect from one firm to another in the same sector. Head-hunting agencies are in the business of inducing executives to do precisely this. Iacocca was a good choice for Chrysler in part because he knew Ford so well. Later when Iacocca was looking for someone to put Chrysler's books in order, he picked a person from a list of Ford finance personnel that he had conveniently taken along with him.

A variation in the recruitment of enemy executives is the notorious "revolving door" syndrome in which public officials leave government posts for jobs in private industries they've been involved in regulating, and vice versa.

Nonetheless, double agentry can have a positive role in politics. In party and factional battles in the U.S. Congress, for instance, each contending camp must locate bipartisan allies who can work in its behalf within the other camp. Such people are essential figures in the process of compromise that is central to the American system of government.

Double agentry may also play a positive role in domestic affairs. Many families have their peacemaker who convinces all parties in a dispute that he or she is on their side and ends up mediating among them all.

One wants to beat, the other is
willing to be beaten.
—*CHINESE SAYING*

STRATAGEM

34 苦肉计

Ku rou ji

*Inflict injury on oneself to win
the enemy's trust*

THIS STRATAGEM rests on the proposition that people tend to feel sympathy for others who suffer misfortune. Even the ruthless Cao Cao could be swayed by the thought of somebody in pain, as the following story shows.

After Zhou Yu had tricked Cao Cao into beheading two generals (as related in the previous stratagem), Zhou Yu became increasingly confident that he could defeat Cao Cao's troops despite their far superior numbers. One of Zhou Yu's best officers, veteran general Huang Gai, challenged this view as unrealistic. Zhou Yu was furious and would have had Huang Gai executed but for the intercession of other officials. Instead Zhou Yu ordered him punished by a hundred lashes, stopping at fifty after others protested again.

That night as the battered Huang Gai lay in his tent, his aide-de-camp Kan Ze crossed the Yangtze and reached Cao Cao's camp, where he was seized by scouts. Kan Ze carried a letter from Huang Gai detailing the general's grievances against Zhou Yu and expressing his desire to defect. Cao Cao did not believe the letter at first, but when informers brought independent news of Huang Gai's beating he finally decided that Huang Gai's maltreatment made his offer believable. Cao Cao welcomed Huang Gai to surrender along with his troops. They reached a secret agreement by which Huang Gai would arrive in boats flying green dragon flags.

Cao Cao did not know that Huang Gai in fact was still loyal to Zhou Yu. Huang Gai's arrival would cause Cao Cao great disaster—a story to be told in the next chapter.

China's historical chronicles and legendary epics contain many other examples of winning trust by self-inflicted injury. An assassin sent to kill China's first emperor, Qin Shihuang, took along the head of his best friend, who was wanted by the emperor, in order to gain an audience. During the Spring and Autumn period, the king of Zheng married off his daughter to the king of Hu and executed an official who advocated invading Hu. Then he launched a surprise attack and conquered Hu. And there are at least two stories of people cutting their own arms off to win an enemy's trust.

This stratagem is practiced in a rather crude way by old-style Chinese street performers who swallow daggers, wind iron bars around their necks, and stick nails into their nostrils before passing around the collection plate.

Chinese students demonstrating in Beijing's Tiananmen Square in the spring of 1989 greatly boosted their movement by inflicting injury upon themselves in the form of a hunger strike. The drama of students fainting, medical workers rushing to the scene, and sirens blaring as ambulances raced up and down the main streets provoked an outpouring of public sympathy. People from all walks of life joined the students, and what had started as marches by several thousand youngsters swelled into crowds of hundreds of thousands—and then an estimated one million for two days in mid-May, upstaging Mikhail Gorbachev's summit with Deng Xiaoping.

A form of self-inflicted injury sometimes seen in the business world is admission of responsibility for a problem or mistake. In mid-1987 when a Chrysler unit and two executives were charged with having sold as new more than 60,000 vehicles that already had been driven with their odometers disabled, Chrysler president Lee Iacocca offered a public apology and extended warranties on the affected cars and trucks. By quickly and openly criticizing himself, he softened the public reaction to the revelation.

In 1987 after *Business Week* magazine disclosed that staff for the discount brokerage firm Charles Schwab and Company had been playing shell games with customer funds, top management immediately took the blame—while claiming ignorance of the activity. Thus a potential volcano was capped.

When hard times befall a company, executives may be able to turn down the heat by assuming some hardship themselves. When Continental Airlines declared bankruptcy in late 1983, chairman Frank Lorenzo slashed his own salary from $257,000 to $43,000 in a show of self-sacrifice. Of course his pay quickly came back up after those employees who were not laid off had accepted wage cuts and Continental had regained its financial health.

In the publishing world it is said that even a pan in the *New York Times* Sunday book review section will sell books. Negative publicity is still publicity. When Jesse Jackson and other black leaders called a press conference to denounce revelations about Martin Luther King's sexual exploits in a new 1989 memoir by another civil rights activist, Reverend Ralph Abernathy, public curiosity increased and the book immediately went into a second printing.

Adversity sometimes breaks careers but other times helps to make them. Young Japanese violinist Midori became an instant celebrity in 1986 after bravely maintaining her composure when strings on two violins she was playing snapped in succession during her premiere performance with the Boston Symphony.

Injury may win sympathy in politics too. Ronald Reagan never intended to get shot, of course—but after he did, his public approval rating soared. Indeed some of his advisers believed the groundswell of public affection that followed John Hinckley's attempt on his life in the spring of 1981 was responsible for the biggest legislative victories of his first term—tax cuts and a budget plan adopted just a few months after the shooting. And the goodwill that followed his recovery from colon cancer surgery in 1985 may have helped him win congressional passage of a tax overhaul bill the subsequent year.

After the 1988 presidential campaign in which Michael Dukakis lost to George Bush, columnist Jeff Greenfield asked Bush's media adviser what would have happened if Dukakis had responded to the Bush campaign's inflammatory ad about furloughed convict Willie Horton by admitting error. Said the media expert, "The issue would have been dead—we would have had to stop raising it. How could we ask people to understand mistakes like Iran-Contra, and then beat Dukakis over the head with the furlough issue if he said he had been wrong?" In other words, inflicting injury upon oneself would have been preferable to merely letting others inflict the injury.

You may find your relationships with others enhanced by injury. Children seem to have an unerring sense of when someone they love is in trouble and will abandon their usual self-centeredness to respond to the difficulty. A vacillating lover may grow more tender if you fall ill. On the other hand, the complications of illness might drive your beloved away. If that's the case, consider yourself lucky—you don't want someone who won't stick around when you need him or her the most.

> When two grasshoppers are tied to
> one string, neither will be able to
> escape.
>
> —CHINESE SAYING

STRATAGEM

35 連環計

Lian huan ji

Chain together the enemy's warships

THIS STRATAGEM focuses on how to transform the opponent's strength into weakness. Chaining ships together means using schemes that will encumber the enemy with his own weight. When this is done successfully, the enemy ends up being his own worst enemy.

The stratagem takes its name from the method by which a small army defeated a far larger one in a battle that took place on the Yangtze River during the Three Kingdoms period. This battle follows the events described in the two previous stratagems, in which Cao Cao was tricked into executing the two generals in charge of naval training for his troops and into accepting another general's defection as genuine.

Cao Cao, leading a force exceeding 800,000 men, still

faced the problem of how to prepare his soldiers for riverine warfare before they crossed the Yangtze in their drive south. The main challenge for these northerners was to overcome their vulnerability to seasickness aboard ship.

Meanwhile, Commander Zhou Yu from the kingdom of Wu, encamped on the south side of the river with a tenth as many troops, was laying plans to destroy Cao Cao's fleet by fire. However, he could not figure out how to make the flames spread, given that the boats were likely to disperse once the fire was set.

Cao Cao thought his problems were over when Pang Tong, a famed military strategist, walked into his tent. Pang Tong was equal in stature to his contemporary Zhuge Liang—at the time, it was said of these two that "whoever can acquire one of them will rule China." Zhuge Liang already was serving Liu Bei, head of the kingdom of Shu, but Pang Tong had not declared his allegiance up to this point. Now he seemed ready and eager to serve Cao Cao. In fact he had decided to help the other side.

After surveying Cao Cao's sturdy, well-ordered fleet and hearing about the northerners' poor constitution, Pang Tong proposed a plan for combating the seasickness problem. He suggested Cao Cao arrange all his vessels, large and small, in rows of thirty or fifty, chain them together at bow and stern, and lay planks across the adjacent decks. "Even horses will be able to travel on them safely," he said. "With your fleet made fast in this way, you need no longer fear the winds and storms, nor the rising and falling tides."

Cao Cao lost no time in ordering his blacksmiths to forge great chains to fasten the ships together. Once the ships were fixed in rows, Cao Cao went to the riverbank to review his navy. Sure enough, despite a strong northwesterly wind, the vessels with sails hoisted charged through the waves like carriages rolling over dry land. The delighted troops, finally delivered from their misery, drilled vigorously on deck with swords and spears.

A few days later, a wind arose from the southeast. Cao Cao laughed confidently, the wind blowing on his face, as

Cao Cao thinks he's being smart to fix his boats together so his soldiers won't get seasick; but in fact it's all been engineered by his rival Zhou Yu, following the stratagem "chaining the enemy's warships together," so that once the boats are ignited they'll all quickly go up in flames.

he watched the ships at the opposite shore roll and pitch in the waves. Suddenly he realized that some boats were drawing closer. His scouts reported that a score of boats with green dragon flags were headed that way at full sail, and one carried a great banner emblazoned with the name Huang Gai who, as described in the last chapter, was supposed to be defecting from the other camp.

Cao Cao felt even happier until one of his advisers pointed out that there was something fishy about these arriving vessels: if Huang Gai were truly defecting, the ships would be laden with grain and sit deep in the water, but these were floating high. The alarmed Cao Cao mobilized troops to intercept them, but it was too late.

When Huang Gai's flotilla was almost to the north bank, he waved his sword and ignited his own leading ships. The wind pushed the burning boats into Cao Cao's fleet, setting it afire as well. Like a dragon ablaze, the inferno raged more than a hundred miles up and down the north bank where Cao Cao's boats were held hostage by their chains. Nearly all the would-be sailors from the north either were incinerated or jumped overboard and drowned. Cao Cao escaped with only a small cavalry force.

This story shows how something the adversary thinks is a strength may turn out to be a weakness. In this case, chaining the boats together to enable troops to fight on water proved to be the undoing of those very troops. Ironically, the stronger one's opponent appears, the more opportunities may exist for taking advantage of weaknesses. Management of large forces requires complex systems for controlling personnel, supplies, and communications, any of which can contain weak spots vulnerable to attack.

In a twelfth-century battle, Jin dynasty troops expected to gain an easy victory over Song dynasty troops on the basis of a strong cavalry. The Song used guerrilla tactics to harass the Jin forces all day long, and after dark the Song soldiers scattered boiled black beans on the ground, which the Jin's ravenous horses promptly went after. No matter how their riders whipped them, they refused to move on, making the horses and soldiers who were supposed to ensure victory sitting ducks for attack. In another battle during the Tang dynasty, one side let 500 mares in heat loose to distract the other side's steeds.

Sometimes this stratagem takes the form of granting to the adversary something he values that actually burdens him more. During the Warring States period, the army of the kingdom of Zhao once killed 30,000 soldiers from Qi. Zhao returned all the corpses to Qi, which might have been seen as a humanitarian concession. In fact the move harmed Qi by exhausting its resources in funeral ceremonies.

Mao Zedong's strategy of "the countryside surrounding the city" is a good application of chaining the enemy's warships together. After World War II when civil war between the Kuomintang and Communists resumed, Mao voluntarily conceded 105 cities to Chaing Kai-shek. After occupying these cities, Chiang had to deploy troops to guard them, which reduced the number of Kuomintang troops at the battlefront by half, from 117 to 58 divisions.

Nowadays, chaining together warships is sometimes employed in international diplomacy. In early 1989, the United States charged Libya with building a poison-gas plant outside Tripoli, and U.S. jets shot down two Libyan jets over the Mediterranean. Libya chose this time to return the body of a U.S. F-11 pilot lost during the American bombing of Libya three years earlier. What looked like a U.S. triumph was actually a smart public relations move for Libya—an expression of goodwill that probably mitagated American calls for air strikes against the suspected plant.

Politics also provides examples. The Polish Communist Party's sudden turnabout in 1989, which saw legalization of the banned union Solidarity and the admittance of opposition parties into electoral politics, may turn out to be a case of the chaining of ships. Faced with Poland's crippling economic problems, the opposition forces may find themselves taking the heat for things that used to be blamed on the Communists, and what looks like a victory could ultimately give way to a defeat.

A fascinating example of chaining together warships from U.S. domestic politics is the controversy over abortion rights. In a July 1989 ruling that left the landmark *Roe vs. Wade* decision in tatters, the U.S. Supreme Court approved state restrictions on abortion. But just three months later, the pro-choice movement achieved stunning victories in the Florida legislature as well as in Congress, reflecting the legislators' awareness that Americans do not like the government telling them what to do in their private lives. Although some states have gone on to tighten limits on abortions, the fact that others are moving in the opposite direction shows that, ironically, the court's consolidation of the antiabortion position may end up strengthening abortion rights.

In business, companies that declare bankruptcy sometimes try to chain together the warships of their creditors. An extreme example is the case of Jack Stanley's Trans-America Natural Gas Corporation, which filed for reorganization twice and operated under court protection for nine out of a dozen years. Stanley made the bankruptcy proceedings as contentious as possible, bombarding creditors with lawsuits and exhausting their will and financial wherewithal. Meanwhile he expanded his company, making it second only to Exxon among Texas natural-gas producers.

The rebate, one of the most common promotional techniques in modern retailing, is a form of chaining together warships. Consumers more readily buy products associated with rebate offers—but they do not necessarily take the trouble to collect and save the necessary proofs-of-purchase, fill in the proper forms, and mail everything in. What looks like a plus for the consumer is in fact a plum for the company.

In your career, your daily life, and your family and personal relationships, this stratagem can serve as a reminder that what appear to be positive events may also hold the seeds of trouble. A professional achievement may bring the jealousy of colleagues down upon you. A job promotion can entail an added burden of time and responsibility that may disrupt your love life. A bargain on a used car may end up costing you money, time, and frustration when breakdowns occur. But with some cautionary investigation, advance planning, and sensitivity, the potential for problems can be reduced.

STRATAGEM

36 走為上

Zou wei shang

Run away

WHEN ALL ELSE FAILS, run away. This is the last-ditch stratagem.

However, running away does not necessarily mean running away for good. When confronted with an absolutely superior enemy, you may surrender, negotiate a compromise, or retreat. Surrender means total defeat, compromise may be tantamount to half a defeat, but retreat is not defeat at all. You may simply have to retreat in order to be able to advance later on.

Mao Zedong recognized the practicality of this stratagem in his famous principle of engagement in guerrilla warfare: "If the battle can be won, fight it; if not, depart."

Its importance was demonstrated during the late Three Kingdoms period when Zhuge Liang, prime minister and military mastermind for the kingdom of Shu in southwest China, launched a series of six expeditions against the more powerful kingdom of Wei. All six ended unsuccessfully and Zhuge Liang himself died of illness on the front during the sixth without realizing his ambition to unify China, although his offensive maneuvers had at least safeguarded the kingdom of Shu during his lifetime.

What is striking about Zhuge Liang's six expeditions is not the failure of his advances but rather the success of his retreats. Each time he had to move 100,000 troops back through the steep Qinling Mountains to the southwest basin while the much stronger and better-equipped Wei army was doing all it could to annihilate them. It was precisely these masterful retreats that enabled the Shu forces to come back for another try.

Zhuge Liang's first expedition failed after one of his generals lost a strategic spot and his army faced the prospect of being wiped out. At this critical juncture, he fooled his Wei adversary Sima Yi by flinging open the gates to the empty city (described in Stratagem 32) and was able to lead his troops back to Shu.

The second expedition ran into logistical difficulties. Here, Zhuge Liang used the technique known as "thrusting a spear from the rear of the horse," giving a mighty backward thrust to Sima Yi's army before escaping across the mountains.

The third retreat was necessitated when Zhuge Liang fell ill. His troops began by falling back only ten miles a day, luring Sima Yi to follow, and then flanking their pursuers and attacking them. By the time the Shu soldiers made their genuine retreat, Sima Yi didn't dare give chase, and it was five days before he learned that they indeed had run away.

The fourth expedition dealt many blows against the Wei, but Sima Yi stymied a final offensive by using a disgruntled Shu officer to sow discord (the double agentry prescribed by Stratagem 33). Zhuge Liang had disciplined the officer, his logistics chief, for drunkenness and dereliction. The of-

RUN AWAY • 199

ficer then went to Sima Yi, who secretly sent him back to the Shu capital to spread rumors that Zhuge Liang planned to usurp power, and when the rumors reached the ears of the ruler he summoned Zhuge Liang home. Along the retreat route, Zhuge Liang used the tactic of increasing the number of cooking stoves each night to make Sima Yi think he was getting reinforcements, so Sima Yi did not give chase.

On the fifth expedition, Zhuge Liang consolidated a strong offensive position by reaping much of the Wei's own wheat harvest. He also designed a special vehicle to transport grain through winding mountain roads. These efforts came to naught, however, when another senior official who had been derelict in his duties forged an order recalling him to the Shu capital again. This time Zhuge Liang set up an ambush at a narrow mountain pass that constituted the only entrance to the southwest basin. Sima Yi's general and many of his troops fell victim to thousands of arrows shot by continuous-shooting bows, another innovation designed by Zhuge Liang.

One might think that Zhuge Liang's death at the front on his sixth expedition would prevent him from mapping out another beautiful retreat. Amazingly, he conducted his final retreat after his death! The scheme, concocted from his deathbed in consultation with his generals, is described as follows in the classic *Romance of the Three Kingdoms*:

Upon hearing that his adversary had died and that the Shu army was in retreat, Sima Yi immediately and joyously led his army in hot pursuit. Suddenly a cannon boomed from behind a hill, deafening shouts resounded through the air, and the fleeing Shu troops wheeled around to face their pursuers, banners flapping and drums beating. The biggest banner of all bore the legend "Prime Minister of Han and Duke of Wuxiang Zhuge Liang." Beneath it, sitting in a cart surrounded by dozens of senior Shu generals, was Zhuge Liang, dressed in his robe and silk hat and waving his feather fan. The astonished Sima Yi, thinking he must have fallen into another trap, turned his horse around and took flight. Sima Yi's soldiers, shocked out of their wits, abandoned their helmets, spears, and halberds and ran for their lives, many of them crushing one another in the stampede.

In fact, the Zhuge Liang who so terrified Sima Yi was only a lifelike statue, carved even before Zhuge Liang's death to commemorate him. The episode led to the coining of a new phrase to describe a person of unusual talent: "A dead Zhuge can scare away a living Sima."

The Chinese Communists' epic 7,500-mile Long March in the mid-1930s was a masterful and heroic example of running away. After suffering heavy losses in the last of five "encirclement and suppression" campaigns launched by Chiang Kai-shek, Mao broke out of the encirclement and headed north, abandoning his base in the Jinggang Mountains of Jiangxi province. Nine out of ten of those who began the journey died on the way, some in battle, many more of hunger, exposure, and illness. But 30,000 managed to reach their destination on the barren loess plateau of Shaanxi province, where they set up a new base. A decade later after the Japanese had been driven from China, Mao redirected his attentions to the showdown with Chiang. From that point it took only three major campaigns and three years for the Communists to drive the Kuomintang from the mainland.

Running away as a problem-solving technique has its roots in Taoism, which extolls the art of nonaction. Sun Bin, the descendant of Sun Zi who retranscribed *The Art of War*, called this stratagem "temporarily yielding to the mighty." In the last analysis, it represents a transition to a new stage.

Retreating sometimes is more difficult than advancing, as mountain climbers well know. Napoleon found this out when the long retreat from Moscow wiped out nearly all his troops. Failing is easy, but failing gracefully and successfully may be harder than outright success. In business too, shutting down an unprofitable venture or withdrawing an unsuccessful product is not as easy as one might suppose.

Strategic planners are familiar with the concept of barriers to entry, but few have thought about the problem of barriers to exit. Factors that may complicate the extrication process include: First, specialized assets, especially in large, capital-intensive firms, are difficult to place elsewhere and lower the liquidation value of a plant or business. Second, there are fixed costs associated with slowing down and stopping production. These include labor settlements and pension-fund contributions and are complicated by low employee productivity.

Third, strategic considerations may inhibit divestment, as the unprofitable business may still be important to the company's overall success. An exit may hurt the company's image and endanger its access to capital markets. Fourth, the managers' sense of pride, emotional commitment, and personal identification with certain projects may foster reluctance to close down a venture. Finally, there may be regulatory barriers and social pressures against closing plants and laying off workers.

Nonetheless, when failure is a fact retreat may be the only way out—and the sooner the better. Management consultant Tom Peters has advocated "faster failure," meaning that if you are not succeeding at something, you should cut your losses and turn your limited resources to something else. Procter and Gamble had the idea of taking the cookie world by storm with its introduction of Duncan Hines "soft cookies" in 1983. Critics commented, "They feel better than they taste." By the time the company retreated, it had sunk tens of millions of dollars into the endeavor.

Although most people undertake new ventures feeling certain of success, anticipating the possibility of failure may be a good general rule. One way to spread risks is by diversifying. As a Chinese saying goes, "A smart hare has three exits from his burrow." A comparable American saying is "Don't put all your eggs in one basket."

Running away does not have to mean giving up an entire venture, plant, or product; sometimes reduction is the answer. When a Japanese ballpoint-pen manufacturer discovered that pen refills tended to leak after writing about

200,000 characters, it solved the problem by shortening the length of refills to contain only about 200,000 characters worth of ink.

At times running away may be employed to achieve a moral victory. This usage has a long and noble tradition in China, illustrated in the tales of upright officials who dared stand up to their superiors—a sure invitation to being fired. One of the earliest was Qu Yuan, an accomplished poet and adviser to the king of Qu in the third century B.C. Due to the perfidy of a rival, his advice was spurned and he was dismissed from office. Later he made the ultimate self-sacrifice, throwing himself into a river after his efforts to save his home state from its enemies had proved futile and his king had been treacherously killed. Qu Yuan's memory is still commemorated in the yearly dragon boat festival on the fifth day of the fifth lunar month.

Another revered official who virtually asked to be banished was Hai Rui of the Ming dynasty (1368–1644). He was disgraced twice, once for criticizing the emperor and then for offending powerful landlords. The first time he was thrown into prison; the second time he ran away to pursue a tranquil life of painting and writing poetry. He is still lionized today.

Individuals, mass movements, and governments could learn from such examples but seldom bother. When the United States was deep into the morass of the Vietnam War, the folksy senator from Vermont George Aiken once said that his country ought to "declare victory and go home." Surely that would have been preferable to the continued devastation and death that only ended with United States defeat and humiliation anyway. The Chinese student hunger strikers who occupied Beijing's Tiananmen Square in the spring of 1989 likewise might have done better by running away. Had they packed up and returned to their campuses after the two days of massive demonstrations that brought a million sympathizers to the square, their reputation would have been at its highest—and nobody would have been shot. Instead they stayed on and on, even after the government had declared martial law; garbage accumulated in the square, citizens grew tired of the stalemate, tensions mounted, and ultimately troops used their guns.

Running away can be a powerful statement against a situation one abhors. The resignation of André Schiffrin and a crew of other publishing professionals from Pantheon Books in early 1990 to protest what they saw as the sacrifice of quality to a bottom-line mentality drew far more public attention to the issue than "putting up and shutting up" would have—and the furor may serve Schiffrin and his colleagues in good stead should they, as was rumored, try to start a rival publishing firm later on.

But the stratagem of running away of course must be used with care. It should never be undertaken thoughtlessly, or out of the mere impulse to flee. We should regard running away not as a means to escape challenges, but rather as a way to better confront them.

APPENDIX

CHRONOLOGY OF CHINESE DYNASTIES

Xia	21st–16th centuries B.C.
Shang	16th–11th centuries B.C.
Western Zhou	11th century–770 B.C.
Eastern Zhou	770–256 B.C.
Spring and Autumn period	722–481 B.C.
Warring States period	403–221 B.C.
Qin	221–206 B.C.
Western Han	206 B.C.–A.D. 9
Xin	A.D. 9–23
Eastern Han	25-220
Three Kingdoms	220–265
(Wei, Shu, Wu)	
Western Jin	265–316
Eastern Jin	317–420
Northern and Southern	
Dynasties	386–581
(Song, Qi, Liang, Chen	
Northern Wei, Eastern Wei,	
Western Wei, Northern Zhou)	
Sui	581–618
Tang	618–907
Five Dynasties	907–960
(Later Liang, Later Tang,	
Later Jin, Later Han,	
Later Zhou)	
Northern Song	960–1127
Southern Song	1127–1279
Yuan	1279–1368
Ming	1368–1644
Qing	1644–1911

ABOUT THE AUTHOR

GAO YUAN was born in a mountain village in North China in 1952 and attended primary and middle school in a county town, where he experienced the political upheaval of the Cultural Revolution. Subsequently he worked as an army truck driver, a foundry technician, and a journalist. He came to the United States to study in 1982 and earned a master's degree in journalism from the University of California, Berkeley, and an MBA from Stanford University. He now represents a U.S. company in China.